W9-CGL-272

MICHIGAN STATE UNIVERSITY LIBRARY

DEC 21 2023

WITHDRAWN

PLACE IN RETURN BOX to remove this checkout from your record.
TO AVOID FINES return on or before date due.
MAY BE RECALLED with earlier due date if requested.

DATE DUE	DATE DUE	DATE DUE
JAN 0 7 2002 0 2 1 2 0 2		
MAY 0 1 2003 0 5 0 1 0 3		

11/00 c:/CIRC/DateDue.p65-p.14

BIG BROTHER'S
INDIAN PROGRAMS—
WITH
RESERVATIONS

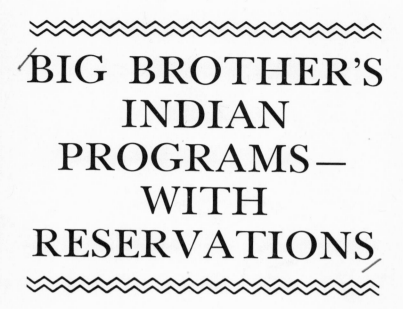

BIG BROTHER'S INDIAN PROGRAMS— WITH RESERVATIONS

BY

Sar A. Levitan

AND

Barbara Hetrick

THE CENTER FOR MANPOWER POLICY STUDIES,
THE GEORGE WASHINGTON UNIVERSITY

McGRAW-HILL BOOK COMPANY

NEW YORK   ST. LOUIS   SAN FRANCISCO   DÜSSELDORF   LONDON
SYDNEY   TORONTO   MEXICO   PANAMA   JOHANNESBURG
KUALA LUMPUR   MONTREAL   NEW DELHI   RIO DE JANEIRO   SINGAPORE

This book was set in Caledonia by University Graphics, Inc.
It was printed on antique paper and bound by Vail-Ballou. The
designer was Christine Aulicino. The editors were Herbert
Waentig, Nancy Tressel, and Laura Givner. Frank Matonti
and Alice Cohen supervised the production.

This volume was prepared under a grant from the Ford Foundation. All photographs are from the Bureau of Indian Affairs.

Copyright © 1971 by McGraw-Hill, Inc.
All Rights Reserved.
Printed in the United States of America.
No part of this publication may be reproduced, stored
in a retrieval system, or transmitted, in any form
or by any means, electronic, mechanical, photocopying,
recording, or otherwise, without the prior
written permission of the publisher.
Library of Congress catalog card number 78-172027
1 2 3 4 5 6 7 8 9   VBVB   7 9 8 7 6 5 4 3 2 1

07-037391-4

E
93
.L66

ß 381813

Contents

Preface

In an age in which public attention is focused upon minority groups, it is only proper that the original Americans who are a minority group in their land would be the subject of widespread public concern. Though Indians claim a uniquely sentimental niche in historical American folklore, they are the most socially and economically disadvantaged population in the entire country.

Volumes have been produced explaining the fascinating intricacies of pottery, legends, religious rites, dress, and customs of Indian Americans. Accounts of the battles between Indians and the United States cavalry, biographies of illustrious warriors, and historical descriptions of tribal life are equally well documented. More recently the vogue has been to denounce the federal government for its mistreatment of our red brothers, and publications devoted to scathing attacks against white society, with appropriate laments for the plight of the poor Indian, have become fashionable. Whatever the accuracy of these charges, even the staunchest advocate of federal programs for Indian Americans must admit that Uncle Sam's big-brother approach has fallen far short of its mark.

This book is concerned only with the delivery of contemporary government programs for residents of Indian reservations. Its primary objective is to study not the Indian people but the federal services designed to enable the first Americans to share in the standard of living which is presumably the birthright of *all* Americans.

Many of the Indian programs are designed especially to

satisfy the needs and conditions peculiar to reservation residents, but they encompass the whole range of federal, social, and welfare activities. The federal government has funded Indian programs to advance the education of their children, improve their health, develop Indian economies, build up the infrastructure of reservations, cultivate their human and natural resources, and much more. Because a single agency, the Bureau of Indian Affairs, has primary responsibility for the welfare of Indian Americans, with supplemental programs scattered among the other executive agencies, this review is organized on a functional, rather than agency, basis.

Beginning with education, which utilizes over a third of the half billion dollars Uncle Sam spends on reservations, this study moves to a discussion of medical care on the reservation. Community organization, welfare, and law and order are considered next, followed by a review of efforts to develop natural, economic, and human resources. The final chapter attempts to indicate the scope and direction that federally supported Indian programs might take in the future.

This volume is an analysis and appraisal of federal assistance to Indians on or near reservations. The study omits discussion of urbanized American Indians even though they may have problems no less pressing than their reservation brothers. It is important to stress that Indians are American citizens who are free to move among the 50 states; indeed, many have done so. Next to the Navajo reservation, with a population of about 120,000, the largest Indian "reservations" are found in Los Angeles, Chicago, and other large metropolitan areas. Besides the problems that face all central city denizens, Indians encounter additional difficulties as immigrants. Thus, the problems of urban Indians are compounded. Having chosen to integrate into the American mainstream, the Indians and their difficulties become part of the complex problems of urban America. Here, however, we are concerned with the provisions made by the federal government for Indians living on or near reservations and Alaskan natives under federal jurisdiction.

The usual lament of a researcher about the inadequacy of data is especially applicable to an evaluation of federal Indian programs. Operational data for the Bureau of Indian Affairs have been scattered among its 11 area offices, and only skimpy composite data on expenditures are maintained by the central office in Washington. Whether the November 1970 announcement concerning the elimination of the area offices will improve BIA data remains to be seen. Recent exercises in connection with the application of the governmental Planning-Programming-Budgeting System have generated new operational data, but these are still in their infancy and of limited help to the evaluator. Other federal agencies have failed to maintain separate information on Indian projects, and the extent of help offered to reservations is unknown. For example, Labor Department manpower officials have only a very vague notion about the amount of funds allocated to projects on or near reservations. Rhetoric about coordinating federal efforts to aid reservations notwithstanding, no reliable estimates are available on the total price tag that can be attached to Big Brother's efforts on behalf of the original Americans.

It would hardly be necessary to mention frustrations of a researcher if they did not have significant policy implications. The correlation between availability of data and the allocation of federal resources remains to be proved, but the appropriation of funds by Congress has frequently depended upon the ability of federal officials to prove the need for funds. It may, therefore, not be at all irrelevant that President Nixon's 1970 message on Indian programs singled out the need of additional funds for health programs but ignored the no less pressing needs for manpower programs. The explanation in assigning priority to health programs above manpower programs may be based on the fact that the Indian Health Service made an eloquent and convincing case for the inadequacy of medical care for Indian Americans, while the Labor Department has failed to indicate the job deficits on Indian reservations, let alone evaluate the impact of its efforts on behalf of Indians.

It is hoped that this review of federal efforts to assist Indians residing on or near reservations will not only help the reader gain a better appreciation of what the government does *to* and *for* Indians but will also assist policy shapers in determining needed priorities in the allocation of resources to Indian reservations.

We are indebted to our associates David Marwick and Robert Taggart III for their help and counsel in preparing this study and to Barbara Ann Pease, who served as administrative assistant on this project. This study would not have been possible without the sustained assistance offered by officials from the Bureau of Indian Affairs, Indian Health Service, and other federal agencies. The help of Roderick H. Riley from the BIA has been particularly valuable. The critical review of the manuscript by Bobbie Kilberg of the White House staff has been most helpful.

This study was prepared under a grant from the Ford Foundation to the George Washington University's Center for Manpower Policy Studies. In accordance with the foundation's practice, complete responsibility for the preparation of the volume was left to the authors.

Sar A. Levitan
Barbara Hetrick

Thanksgiving 1970

BIG BROTHER'S INDIAN PROGRAMS— WITH RESERVATIONS

"MAY THE GREAT SPIRIT SHED LIGHT ON YOURS, AND THAT YOU MAY NEVER EXPERIEN(
THE HUMILIATION THAT THE POWER OF THE AMERICAN GOVERNMENT HAS REDUCED N
TO, IS THE WISH OF HIM WHO, IN HIS NATIVE FORESTS, WAS ONCE AS PROUD AS YOU."
BLACK HAWK

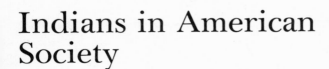

Chapter 1

Indians in American Society

WHO ARE THE INDIANS?

Most Americans have acquired their awareness about the native Indian population from fragmentary and cursory school discussions or from television westerns. Both of these sources have contributed to vague and distorted views about American Indians. Even though the days of marauding braves attacking forts and white settlements are in the past (if they ever existed), the image persists of Indians living on their own reservations, weaving rugs in front of buffalo skin tepees, herding sheep, and continuing their "quaint" old way of living amid majestic mountains and painted deserts.

As with most myths, there is an element of truth in this picture. The majority of those who claim to be of Indian descent continue to live on or near reservations specifically designated for them by the United States government. However, many who live on reservations are not native to the areas they inhabit because their ancestors were forced into these Indian enclaves by the conquering white settlers.

The image of the subdued and "pacified" Indian living

Top: *Navajo matron spinning yarn from wool she has just carded, all in the process of weaving a rug which she has begun on the loom behind her.* Bottom: *Substandard housing on Sioux reservation.*

off the beaten track has been marred in recent years. As the civil rights movement reached both reservation Indians and their urban brothers, advocates of "Red Power" have adopted the increasing militancy of repressed minorities in seeking greater freedom and self-determination for Indians. Manifestations of this newly aroused sentiment include the Indian occupation of Alcatraz Island, the seizure of Ellis Island, and the march on Fort Lewis.

On a different level, experts find it difficult to identify the American Indians, and there is no universally accepted legal definition of an American Indian. Thus, government agencies have used different measures of identification, depending upon their assigned functions and reflecting their reasons for counting the Indian population. For example, the Bureau of the Census, which is charged with the constitutional requirement of enumerating the American population, relies upon the individual counted to identify himself as Indian. The 1970 questionnaire did not spell out who was "qualified" to be an Indian and allowed the individual respondent to decide his own race; moreover, Indian respondents were requested to indicate their tribe. For purposes of decennial counting, the Bureau of the Census approach is probably more accurate and more satisfactory than any other method.

Other government agencies, however, could not accept self-definition because eligibility to participate in federal programs and services is normally determined by statutes or treaties. These statutes are typically designed to fulfill obligations assumed by the United States when the Indians were forced to accept reservations of land in return for their "safety." During nearly two centuries of U.S. history, the government has passed numerous laws affecting Indians, presumably meant to provide for the descendants of the original native population. For example, Congress appropriates funds specifically to educate Indian children and to provide health services for the Indian population, and certain lands are owned in perpetuity by Indians of specified tribes. But beginning with the offspring of Pocahontas, it became increasingly difficult to separate Indians from more recent arrivals to this continent. While this did not discourage Congress from passing Indian laws, the federal agencies administering them understandably did not allow the individual to determine his entitlement to specified rights and services. Instead, eligibility under Indian laws was made dependent upon being half Indian or quarter Indian or being listed on a tribal roll. The Bureau of Indian Affairs (BIA), the oldest and major federal agency dealing with Indians, provides services to Indians who are the beneficial owners of reservation or other trust lands. Typically, these Indians are members or heirs of members of tribal organizations having a special treaty or agreement with the federal government or for whom statutes have been enacted. But for applicants for educational assistance, seekers of land titles, and persons otherwise applying individually for a BIA service, proof of Indian "blood" is generally necessary.

Further delineating their service population, the Bureau describes a reservation as a block of tribally owned land, areas of land allotted to individual tribal members, and interspersed land belonging to non-Indians. Today, many reservations contain little tribal land, and a major portion of total acreage may have passed out of even individual Indian ownership, but they continue to be treated as "reservations." Technically, trusts or restricted areas of land owned by Indians within the boundaries of former reservations in Oklahoma, some small ranches and colonies set aside for use by Indians, and native communities located on restricted land in the state of Alaska are not reservations. Nevertheless, the BIA treats those living within these land areas as reservation residents. Employing a bit of reverse logic, the BIA conversely defines reservations as "units of land, large or small, which are subject to some degree of administration by the Bureau."[1]

The Indian Health Service (IHS) of the Department of Health, Education, and Welfare, second only to the Bureau of Indian Affairs in responsibility for Indian welfare, also defines its own service population but generally adheres to similar standards as the BIA.[2] The Indian Health Service's responsibility encompasses a greater number of Indians than the Bureau of Indian Affairs' direct services, because the IHS generally allows individual reservations and communities to decide who is eligible for federal health care services. This discretion tends to swell the service population.

And there are still other definitions. The Department of Health, Education, and Welfare considers an Indian one who "is regarded as an Indian by the community in which he lives as evidenced by such factors as membership in a tribe, residence on tax-exempt land, ownership of restricted property, and active participation in tribal affairs." The Code of Federal Regulations stipulates that states may receive educational assistance for public school students with a minimum of one-quarter Indian "blood," and membership in a tribe is required of one or both parties for matters concerning tribal law and order. The Indian Reorganization Act of 1934 allows tribes to define Indian identity for themselves. Some tribes have accepted the opinion of individuals; some require recognition by the community; and others require Indian "blood" or merely accept the Bureau of the Census definition. While most tribes require one-quarter Indian descent for federal programs, the Five Civilized Tribes (Cherokees, Chickasaws, Choctaws, Creek, and Seminoles) have decided by tribal resolution that an individual must have at least one-half Indian blood to be eligible for federal programs.

Certainly the confusion over who is to be regarded as

an Indian has contributed to inconsistencies in population and program data.[3]

The Indian Claims Commission established by Congress in 1946 to adjudicate claims against the United States by any "identifiable group of American Indians" is not concerned with the claimant's residence. Once a claim is determined to be proper, the members of the tribe or band or their descendants are entitled to compensation even if they have left the reservation.

Most official definitions of an Indian are contrived at best and are usually the product of congressional action. What is most significant—and the Census Bureau comes closest to recognizing this fact—is how an individual is perceived by both himself and his community. It is quite conceivable that a person with less than one-quarter Indian blood could be accepted by tribesmen and ostracized by whites in a given community, while a full blood could live in an eastern metropolis as a fully assimilated white. This consideration makes it easier to understand why estimates of the total American Indian population range from one-half million to more than twice that number.

It is not surprising, therefore, that there is no single authoritative counting of the Indian population. In its 1970 decennial census, the Bureau of the Census counted a total of 792,000 Indians in the United States, the majority living in rural areas and for the most part on reservations. These data are of limited use to the Bureau of Indian Affairs and other agencies. Legislation has demanded that the BIA's prime concern be with Indians living on or near reservations and other "officially" recognized Indian enclaves. This, of course, excludes Indians who migrate to urban areas. For example, next to the Navajo reservation, the single largest concentration of Indians is in Los Angeles. By counting only reservation Indians living on or adjacent to reservations, the BIA estimated in 1970 the total Indian population

entitled to its services to be 478,000, but this number included all Alaskan natives because the term "adjacent" in
this case encompasses all Alaska. On the other hand, the
BIA counts Oklahoma Indians who live on former reservations as its clients. Nearly nine of every ten Indians that
the BIA considers in its jurisdiction live in nine states (Table
1). The largest Indian concentration, 115,000, is found in
Arizona; next are Oklahoma, 81,000; New Mexico, 77,000;
and Alaska, 57,000. Only five other states had over 10,000
Indians living on or adjacent to reservations.

There is also a discrepancy in the counting of reservations.
According to one BIA official, there was a total of 270
reservations, 24 other scattered land areas maintained in
federal trusteeship for Indians, Eskimos, and Aleuts, and
over 100 government-owned areas used by Indians and
native people in Alaska.[4] But another BIA publication states
that there were 290 Indian reservations in 1968.[5] Indicative
of this general confusion even within the BIA is the recent
"discovery" that the Ozette reservation in the state of Washington, "established" for no apparent reason in 1893 (its
inhabitants were actually members of the nearby Makah

Table 1. Estimates of Indian Population on or Adjacent to
Federal Reservations, Total and Selected States, March 1970

STATE	POPULATION
Total	478,000
Arizona	115,000
Oklahoma*	81,000
New Mexico	77,000
Alaska †	57,000
South Dakota	30,000
Montana	23,000
Washington	16,000
North Dakota	14,000
Minnesota	11,000
All other states	54,000

* Includes former reservation areas in Oklahoma.
†Includes all Indians and Alaskan natives.
Source: Bureau of Indian Affairs.

reservation), has been deserted since 1908. A bill to make this land part of the Makah reservation has been introduced in Congress; thus another reservation "bit the dust."[6]

There is no single, typical residential pattern among American Indians: some tribes group into small villages; some tribes scatter themselves with miles between neighbors; others live in towns or familial groups or tribal enclaves of greatly varying populations. By far the largest and most highly populated reservation is the Navajo, which spans part of Arizona, New Mexico, and Utah and covers an area the size of West Virginia. About 120,000 Navajos live on this reservation. At the other extreme are nearly 100 tribes. with fewer than 100 persons each (Table 2). Many tribes are located near large cities, but more reside in isolated rural regions where there is no easily accessible transportation to urban areas. The 300 separate languages spoken by American Indians are evidence that these communities contain members whose mores, values, and culture vary as considerably among themselves as they do from other ethnic groups and the dominant white society.

* A review of demographic characteristics shows Indians to be a comparatively young and growing population. Despite

Table 2. Number of Indian Reservations by Size of Population, 1969

POPULATION SIZE	TOTAL POPULATION	NUMBER OF RESERVATIONS
Total	456,520	255
Less than 100	3,105	78
100–499	19,635	75
500–999	18,328	25
1,000–1,999	44,717	32
2,000–4,999	74,897	23
5,000–9,999	103,347	15
10,000–19,999	70,946	6
20,000–49,999	—	—
Over 50,000	121,545	1

Note: Over 100 Alaskan villages are administratively grouped into five agencies. These agencies are treated as reservations in this table.
Source: Bureau of Indian Affairs, *Labor Force Reports*, March 1969.

a mortality rate higher than the national average, an un-
usually high birth rate is causing the Indian population to
increase by 3 percent annually—a rate which is twice the
national rate of natural increase. Whereas the average age
at death for American Indians is 44, compared with 64 for
the remainder of the population, the Indian birthrate (37.4
per 1,000 population) is over twice that of the rest of the
country.[7]

Because Indians die younger and relatively more are born,
their population is relatively young. The median age of
Indians living on or adjacent to reservations is only 17
years, compared with a median age of about 29 for the rest
of the nation.

From all indications, it appears that the Indian population
will continue to increase in the near future. If current preventive health and medical care programs reduce Indian
death rates, especially in the younger age groups, the immediate effect will be a lowering of the death rate at all ages.
While the increase in persons in the older age cohorts will
tend to level the death rate and eventually decrease the
birthrate, it will contribute to the rapid net growth in
population.[8]

SOCIOECONOMIC CONDITIONS

Although there is little agreement about the appropriate
means of delivering assistance, the case for expending additional aid to Indians living on reservations is indeed persuasive. The single most salient indicator of their desperate
need for assistance is their comparatively low income. While
such factors as level of education, rate of employment, and
state of health are significant contributors to a group's
opportunity for adequate living conditions, secure status
in society, and control over life chances, they are neither
necessary nor sufficient. An adequate level of income, on
the other hand, *is* necessary and generally sufficient to

assure the "good life," including health, balanced diet, adequate housing, good education, and the other amenities of life.

But Indians have been denied the opportunity to achieve a proper share of these goods and services. The average per capita cash income for Indians on or near reservations was only $900 in 1968, less than one-third of the national average. According to a Bureau of Indian Affairs survey of 113 reservations containing three-fourths of the BIA service population, two-thirds lived on reservations where the per capita income was less than $1,000. On only four reservations, with a combined population of less than 2,000, did per capita income equal or exceed the national average of $3,420 (Table 3). Among these were the 115 members of the Agua Caliente reservation in California whose per capita income was $18,225, almost entirely earned as property income. Long ago, in 1894, this tribe was allowed to establish title to some desert land which is now Palm Springs.

The median family income of Indians on the reservations surveyed by the Bureau of Indian Affairs was $3,600, while the Bureau of the Census reports that whites and all non-white families earned $8,937 and $5,141, respectively, in 1968. And nearly three-fifths of Indian households, but only 14 percent of white families and 36 percent of non-

Table 3. Distribution of Per Capita Income by Reservations, 1968

PER CAPITA INCOME	NUMBER OF RESERVATIONS	POPULATION
Total	113	356,495
Less than $500	10	8,682
$500–749	32	179,995
$750–999	23	55,061
$1,000–1,249	21	80,171
$1,250–1,749	16	25,313
$1,750 or more	11	7,273

Source: Bureau of Indian Affairs.

white families, had an income below $4,000. The lower family income of reservation families must be shared with larger-than-average families, for it is estimated that Indian households are composed of between four and five persons and that the national average is 3.2 members per household (Table 4).

Table 4. Distribution of Families by Income, 1968

	MEDIAN	UNDER $3,000 (in percentages)	$3,000–3,999 (in percentages)	$4,000 OR MORE (in percentages)
White	$8,937	9	5	85
Nonwhites	5,360	24	12	64
Indians*	3,600	42	15	43

* Estimated from medians and distributions of households on 113 reservations.
  Source: For Indians, Bureau of Indian Affairs, Summary of Reservation Development Studies, 1969. For others, Bureau of the Census, Current Population Reports, ser. P-60, no. 66.

Differences in the sources of personal income between reservation Indians and the national population further illustrate the Indians' economic deprivation (Table 5). Nearly one-third of the very low earned Indian income came from antipoverty, welfare, and other government programs,

Table 5. Sources of Personal Income for United States and 113 Indian Reservations, 1968

	RESERVATIONS		UNITED STATES
	IN MILLIONS	PERCENT	PERCENT
Total personal income	$319.5	100.0	100.0
Earned income	267.3	83.7	91.4
Wages, salaries, and other labor income*	223.1	69.8	67.8
Proprietors and other nonlabor income †	44.2	13.8	23.6
Transfer payments	52.2	16.3	8.6

* Less personal contributions for social insurance.
† Includes farm income, business and professional income, rental income of persons, dividends, and personal interest income.
Note: Details may not add because of rounding.
Source: Bureau of Indian Affairs and U.S. Department of Commerce.

compared with less than 15 percent from these sources nationally. And one-sixth of their income, or twice the national proportion of 8.5 percent, was derived from transfer payments.

Property income amounted to approximately 14 percent on reservations, but 24 percent nationally. The most glaring difference is found in commercial and industrial activity, which is the source of only 14 percent of reservation personal income. Nationally, manufacturing, trade, and services (a category that is less inclusive than the reservation "commercial and industrial" classification) constitute about 40 percent of personal income (Table 6).

Certainly, chronically depressed economic conditions and low wages, even where jobs are available, are major contributors to widespread Indian poverty. The average unemployment rate on Indian reservations is normally higher than unemployment rates in even the most depressed city slum areas.

This job deficit and low income are further reflected in deplorable housing conditions. Nearly four of every five Indian families live in unsanitary, dilapidated housing, compared with 8 percent of all American families living in inadequate houses. Though funding of public housing by the federal government was initiated during the 1930s, a quarter century elapsed before the federal government began to take steps to alleviate the poor housing on Indian reservations.

Moreover, poverty and substandard housing conditions are reflected in the serious health deficiencies suffered by American Indians. The average infant mortality rate among Indians is 1½ times that of the rest of the population, and the life expectancy of those who do survive is much lower than that of either the white or black populations. The average age at the time of death for an Indian (44) is two decades younger than it is for the average American (64). Poverty and its symptoms of poor diets and unsanitary living

Table 6. Distribution of Personal Income on 113 Reservations by Source, 1968

Total personal income (percent)	100.0
Earned income	83.7
Forest	4.8
Rangeland	9.2
Dry farm: pasture	3.3
Irrigated land	4.2
Minerals	2.1
Commercial and industrial	14.1
Government	29.2
BIA	9.8
Indian Health Service	3.8
Economic Opportunity Act	6.7
Other federal	2.4
State and county	2.1
Tribe	4.3
Outdoor recreation	0.5
Other leased	7.2
All off-reservation	8.9
Transfers	16.3
Welfare	10.7
Public assistance	7.2
BIA assistance	1.9
Other assistance	0.6
Unemployment compensation	1.0
Other transfers	5.6
OASDI	4.3
VA	0.6
Other cash	0.7

Source: Bureau of Indian Affairs.

conditions have contributed to a widespread incidence of disease caused by malnutrition.

LEGAL STATUS

Indians were granted full citizenship in 1924, and they live in all the 50 states. Nonetheless, most Indians tend to concentrate in several western states on or near reservations set aside for them by the federal government. As the white settlers pushed westward, they forced Indians into specified areas of land, a nineteenth century version of concentration camps. While some Indians were assigned to reservations in their native areas, many others were forced to march long distances from their native habitat to specially designated areas.

Having forced most American Indians onto reservations, the government next formulated a policy of assimilating them into American society. This was to be achieved under the terms of the new settlers, and the Indians were to forsake their religious practices, social organizations, and other elements of native culture. Modern preoccupation with appropriate length of male hair is not new. The dominant American society a century ago thought they could "help" Indians assimilate by requiring them to adopt the tonsorial fashions and language of the new settlers, and this emphasis persisted vigorously through the 1930s. In brief, Indians were considered wards of the state and were treated under the law as incapable of making their own decisions. Indians were often forbidden to leave their reservations without prior clearance.

The forced melting pot policy did not work. Indians refused to be melted because white society offered no viable alternative to their existing culture. While many Indians intermarried and the number of descendants who now inhabit the 50 states is not known, there remain some 312 distinct tribal communities speaking 300 languages and living on nearly 300 reservations.

There was an economic basis in the desire to assimilate the Indians. So long as land was plentiful, Indians were allowed to keep a total of some 22,000 square miles (140 million acres). Though the land assigned for Indian reservations accounted for less than 1 percent of the total land mass of the continental United States, the new settlers coveted it. If the Indians were assimilated, then presumably their land could be absorbed as well.

THE DAWES ACT

In response to white demand for takeover of reservation land, new legislation reduced Indian land holdings. The policy of forced assimilation culminated with the General Allotment Act of 1887 (the Dawes Act), which authorized the President to divide tribal land into individual tracts of 40, 80, or 160 acres, to be used strictly for agricultural and grazing purposes.[9] These tracts were to be allotted to families or individuals while the federal government retained title for 25 years or longer, after which the allottee would receive a fee patent enabling him to use or dispose of the land as he saw fit, subject to state and territorial laws. Upon receiving a patent, the individual was to become a voting citizen if he maintained residence apart from his tribe.

The rationale behind the Dawes Act was that an Indian who possessed land would automatically become a farmer and that a farming Indian would naturally become "civilized" and self-supporting. Farmers, of course, needed less land than did tribal hunters and fishermen, so surplus land was made available for purchase by whites. The government ignored the protests of Indians against land allotment, a practice contrary to their tradition of communal property rights. Undesirous of private ownership, unfamiliar with farming as a way of life, and lacking the provisions for agricultural training and the credit with which to purchase livestock and farming implements, Indians lost their land. Acreage owned by Indians dropped from 140 million acres to 78 million in 1900 and to about 55 million acres by 1934 when the process of allotment was finally discontinued by statute.

INDIAN REORGANIZATION ACT

In an attempt to repair damages incurred under the Dawes Act, Congress passed the Indian Reorganization Act of 1934.

While the new law did not abandon the principle of assimilation as national policy, it did allow for a more gradual process. By recognizing the value of Indian communal organization for social control and progress, the act permitted tribes to reorganize their own institutions and manage their own affairs. Individual rights were also expanded. Provisions were made to permit Indians to purchase land, establish chartered business organizations, and become eligible for BIA employment without regard to civil service regulations.

Colonialism was not abandoned, however, and the BIA retained veto power over most tribal decisions, especially those pertaining to financial matters. Whatever the intent of the Reorganization Act, BIA officials continued business as usual and did little to help tribes form self-sustaining communities. Reservations remained under the complete dominance of Washington-appointed officials.

Morever, the passage of the Reorganization Act was followed by more than three very lean decades for the country's reservations. Indians suffered even more from the Great Depression than did other ethnic groups, despite special relief such as CCC employment in forestry and "rehabilitation" housing. And while Indian manpower was used in both the armed services and defense industries during the Second World War, this increase in employment was accompanied by severe cutbacks in appropriations for social services, health, education, and land purchases.

TERMINATION

The obviously pressing need following World War II was to compensate for the appropriations to Indians which were cut back during the Great Depression and World War II.
Disregarding the long history of dependency that was forced upon reservation Indians and the depletion of tribal resources, Congress, with the support of officials administering

Indian programs in the executive agencies, released the government even further from responsibility for Indians by terminating federal responsibility. In 1953 Congress passed a resolution (House Concurrent Resolution 108) calling for termination of federal supervision of reservations in five states and seven additional locations. Termination was to occur as expeditiously as possible. Indian protests were again ignored, and BIA responsibility for several tribes, including the Klamath of Oregon, the tribes of western Oregon, the Menominee tribe of Wisconsin, and six tribes in Utah—totalling about 10,000 Indians in all—was consequently terminated.

Controversy over termination continues. The disastrous impact of the sudden termination of reservations without providing the necessary infrastructure to support their residents left few supporters of termination among Indians or government officials in the BIA and other agencies. Members of Congress, ex-Secretary of Interior Hickel, ex-President Johnson, and most recently President Nixon, have indicated their opposition to termination. The Nixon administration policy was announced in a Presidential message on July 8, 1970, repudiating the termination policy adopted by Congress in 1953 and continued until at least 1958. The newly announced policy recognized that before federal support is removed from a reservation, there is a need to guarantee that the residents will be given the opportunity to form their own government and to control their own institutions. Obviously, this requires that Indian tribes be provided with the necessary resources to make self-support possible. It is hoped that the future will see all tribes and the federal government working together to achieve independence for the Indians. The first Americans should have the opportunity to choose whether they want to become assimilated, whether they want to maintain their Indian heritage, or whether they prefer to select the best from both cultures and be comfortable and accepted in both.

TRIBAL GOVERNMENT

The government of American Indians living on reservations is the product of literally thousands of treaties, federal laws, and judicial decisions, and myriad rules and regulations issued by federal agencies over more than a century and a half. Indian trust land designated as reservations is free from state and local taxation, and the federal government is charged with the responsibility of providing educational, health, and other social services for the welfare of reservation Indians where states do not meet these needs. Because Indians are subject to federal laws detailed in treaties and other arrangements, the jurisdictional power of states over reservations is circumscribed.

Whatever the intent and content of the several hundred original treaties with American Indians may have been, reservation tribes historically have been treated as unconditionally surrendered nations. Tribal governments are supposed to maintain autonomy over their affairs unless explicitly circumscribed by Congress. In reality, the federal government reserves the right to veto all tribal laws, codes, ordinances, and financial arrangements. While Congress uses the rhetoric of giving Indians freedom of action, it also empowers the Secretary of the Interior to regulate in utmost detail the administration of federal programs for the Indians, a mandate which the federal officials exercise with great diligence. This denies reservation Indians control not only over their educational, social, and welfare institutions, but also over their own resources. Only recently have a few tribes, namely, the Pima Maricopa in Arizona and the Zuñi Pueblos in New Mexico, begun to take over BIA functions. Paternalism of the federal government is extended to control over the expenditures of funds collected by Indian tribes through the sale of reservation products or leasing of reservation land.

The underlying basis of federal officials' long arm over Indian affairs is a bureaucratic inclination to play it safe and ensure that federal funds are not misappropriated and that federal "guardianship" responsibilities are fully exercised. Federal officials insist that, except for exercising their proper function of representing the United States government, they permit Indians to elect their own tribal governments, adopt and operate their own polity, control the behavior of their constituents, tax aliens conducting business on land within their jurisdiction, and administer justice through their own courts. In law, too, the fiction of Indian self-government persists. According to a 1959 decision of the United States Court of Appeals, "Indian tribes . . . have a status higher than that of States."[10] The effectiveness of this internal self-government, however, is necessarily extremely circumscribed by the fact that control over tribal resources is still maintained by federal officials.

It was inevitable that the social upheavals of the 1960s, with their concomitant emphasis on securing rights for minorities, also reached Indian reservations. Black militancy brought in its wake increased assertiveness on the part of browns and reds to demand equal rights. While new institutions were necessary to help blacks gain control over the social institutions affecting their lives, Indian tribal governments at first appeared to supply the natural instrument for self-government and control over the Indians' own destinies. Even when the federal bureaucracies were ready to respond to pressure and permit Indians greater control over their own institutions, it did not follow that tribal establishments were any more ready to relinquish their powers than political entities in other American communities. Nonetheless, in an era of participatory democracy, a trend toward greater self-government is nearly inevitable; traditional federal policies that specify what is good for the Indians without allowing the Indians to help determine governmental policies or programs affecting their lives are bound to change.

It should not be at all surprising that Indians as a group lack clear-cut and easy solutions to these complex problems. And most Indian spokesmen speak with a "forked tongue" about the future direction and appropriate policies that society should adopt toward the "Indian problem." Dependent as the reservations are upon Washington's largesse, Indian spokesmen raise the slogans of self-determination while deploring any suggestions that the Bureau of Indian Affairs and other federal agencies terminate their responsibilities for Indians living on or near reservations. It takes little imagination or creative social thinking to attack federal officialdom for its colonialism, but it is an entirely different ball game to design a viable plan which would enable Indian tribes to become self-sufficient communities without depending upon Washington for basic services.

What, then, is the answer to the "Indian problem"? Indians and bureaucrats alike have generally abandoned the notion of assimilating the Indian into the American melting pot. The record indicates that Indians refuse to be melted. Spokesmen for the first Americans say they want—and the Washington agencies profess to echo their desire—to maintain the best of their own heritage while simultaneously taking advantage of all the best that white society has to offer. So far no one has been able to derive a formula for the realization of this goal. Indians have been no more able to share the affluent American standard of living and still retain the traditional tribal ways of life than the farmer has preserved the colonial style of living in the complex world of contemporary America.

Tribal traditionalists assume a posture of "wait and see," for the Indians have managed to hold onto their identity despite centuries of subordination and aborted attempts to destroy their culture. Others are willing to accommodate both white and Indian cultures, but they admit to finding no acceptable method of doing so. Increasingly vociferous

are the "Red Power" militants who demand that the United
States increase spending for education, roads, housing, and
health as compensation for stolen land and broken treaties.
Although they want freedom from federal regulations and
unsolicited advice, they, too, are unsure of the direction
they want their future to take. This is not intended to deny
the possibility of improving the Indian situation, but simply
to suggest that there is no single or simple solution to the
current dilemma.

SCOPE

Federal programs for Indians are designed to enable the
first Americans to share in the standard of living which is
presumably the birthright of *all* Americans. It goes without
saying that this should be achieved under maximum conditions of self-determination. Altogether, the allocation of
federal dollars to Indians living on or near reservations
doubled during the decade of the 1960s and is still rising.
Federally supported programs range from birth-control
projects to providing assistance for the aged; from building
homes to building roads, schools, and factories; from support-
ing health clinics to constructing community buildings
(Table 7).

      This volume is an analysis and appraisal of federal assis-
tance to Indians on or near reservations. The study omits
discussion of urbanized American Indians even though they
may have problems no less pressing than their reservation
brothers. It is important to stress that Indians are American
citizens who are free to move among the 50 states; indeed,
many have done so. Next to the Navajo reservation, with a
population of about 120,000 persons, the largest Indian
"reservations" are found in Los Angeles, Chicago, and other
large metropolitan areas. In addition to the problems that
face all central-city denizens, Indians face additional dif-

Table 7. *Estimated Federal Expenditures for Reservation Programs, Fiscal 1970*

PROGRAM	AMOUNT (MILLIONS)
Total	$538.2
Education	191.7
Federal schools	135.3
Public schools	38.5
Head Start	10.2
Other	7.7
Health	109.5
Direct patient care	56.8
Contract patient care	20.1
Field health	26.6
Other	6.0
Community organization	12.2
Housing	14.6
Welfare and social services (BIA only)	24.7
Claims and awards	22.9
Economic and resources development	93.8
Agricultural and industrial assistance	38.7
Road construction and maintenance	24.6
Building construction and maintenance (other than school)	6.3
Forest lands and other resources	24.2
Manpower	58.8
Direct employment	11.8
Adult vocational training	21.6
Adult education	3.6
Other manpower programs	21.8
Miscellaneous	10.0

Note: Table does not include income maintenance and other outlays unrelated to reservation programs.

Source: Participating government agencies.

ficulties as immigrants. Thus, the problems of urban Indians are compounded. Having chosen to integrate into the American mainstream, the Indians and their difficulties become part of the complex problems of urban America. Here, however, we are concerned with the provisions made by the federal government for Indians living on or near reservations and Alaskan natives under federal jurisdiction. While federal

funds are distributed among various agencies, over half of
the available money is given to the Bureau of Indian Affairs
of the Department of the Interior.

The BIA has primary responsibility for the welfare of the
nation's Indians. It is charged with protecting their resources,
administering most social services not offered by the states,
constructing necessary facilities, and assisting them to
develop their potential. While the other government agencies
with programs designed to benefit Indians may concentrate
upon a single service or activity, the Bureau's realm of
responsibility encompasses all those functions necessary to
satisfy the nation's debts to the American Indian and implement administrative and legislative measures.

While the Continental Congress established an office for
Indian affairs, the BIA was not established until 1824, and
the Office of Commissioner of Indian Affairs was not created
by Congress for another eight years. Because white settlements near Indian country consisted primarily of Army
outposts, the Bureau was under the direction of the Secretary
of War and subject to regulations directly prescribed by the
President until its transfer to the newly established Department of the Interior in 1849. This transfer of authority from
a military to a civilian institution had little effect upon the
delivery of services since military personnel maintained a
monopoly on BIA field positions for many years following
the change.

For more than a century, the BIA remained the sole agency
directly responsible for the welfare of reservation Indians.
In 1955, responsibility for health care was removed from the
BIA and transferred to the Division of Indian Health of the
Department of Health, Education, and Welfare's Public
Health Service. With the expansion of antipoverty programs
during the 1960s, other agencies extended their activities
onto reservations. Poverty-ridden Indian enclaves were a
natural target for Office of Economic Opportunity activities,

and the Economic Development Administration, concerned with rejuvenating depressed areas, made special efforts to bring industry to Indian reservations. The Labor Department stepped in to help train Indians to fill the newly expanded job market on or near reservations. The Department of Housing and Urban Development has taken steps to upgrade the physical living conditions on reservations.

The proliferation of federal programs, as usual, brought a clamor for coordinating the various efforts. This was to be accomplished by establishing a new federal unit at the summit—the National Council on Indian Opportunity (NCIO), headed by the Vice President. Neither of the two most recent Vice Presidents has assigned a high priority to his task of heading the NCIO. A careful investigator would be hard put to find any actual achievements of the Council.

The present discussion is organized on a functional rather than on an organizational basis. Starting with education, which utilizes nearly a third of the total funds allocated for Indians, it moves to a discussion of medical care on reservations. Welfare is considered next, followed by an analysis of resource utilization and economic development. The final chapter is an attempt to indicate a direction that federally supported Indian programs might take in the future.

NOTES

1. U.S. Department of the Interior, Bureau of Indian Affairs, *U.S. Indian Population (1962) and Land (1963)*, November 1963, p. 2. (Mimeographed.)

2. Jean Nowak, "What's Happening With the Indians," *Health Services and Mental Health Administration World,* September–October 1969, p. 30.

3. Steve Langone, "A Statistical Profile of the Indian: The Lack of Numbers," in *Toward Economic Development for Native American Communities,* Joint Economic Committee, 91st Cong., 1st Sess., 1969, p. 5.

4. Bill King, "Some Thoughts on Reservation Economic Development," in ibid., p. 68.

5. "Answers to Your Questions About American Indians," U.S. Government Printing Office, 1968, p. 15.

6. "Lands Held by United States in Trust for Makah Indian Tribe, Washington," *Congressional Record,* daily ed., July 6, 1970, p. H6336.

7. U.S. Department of Health, Education, and Welfare, Public Health Service, *Indian Health Trends and Services,* 1969, p. 2.

8. J. Nixon Hadley, "The Demography of the American Indians," *The Annals of the American Academy of Political and Social Science,* May 1957, p. 30.

9. Act of February 8, 1887, 24 Stat. 388.

10. *Native American Church v. Navajo Tribal Council,* 1960.

"NOW WE SHALL NOT REST UNTIL WE HAVE REGAINED OUR RIGHTFUL PLACE. WE SHALL TELL OUR YOUNG PEOPLE WHAT WE KNOW. WE SHALL SEND THEM TO THE CORNERS OF THE EARTH TO LEARN MORE. THEY SHALL LEAD US." — DECLARATION OF THE FIVE COUNTY CHEROKEES

Chapter 2

Little Change in the Classroom

HISTORICAL REVIEW

Ever since the white man first settled on the American continent, he has considered it his god-given mission to transform the first Americans into the image of the new settlers. The new arrivals simply assumed their culture to be superior to that of the native inhabitants and consequently decided that the best way to "help" the Indian was to inculcate the latter with the values and style of the European way of life.

Because the older natives were too "set in their ways," the salvation (which the settlers equated with assimilation) of the Indians was to come through the education of their children. But agreeing on a goal did not necessarily involve consensus on the means by which they would achieve the desired end. This question of methods raised in colonial days persists to the present day. The issue of the relevancy of education is not a new discovery of today's college students; it was raised by Indian leaders over two centuries ago. In the process of negotiating a treaty in 1744 with six Indian tribes, the leaders of Virginia offered to educate one Indian youth from each of the tribes. The Indian chiefs respectfully rejected the

Top: *Young builders of the Pima-Maricopa tribe on the Salt River reservation in Arizona learn cooperation, as part of the tribally sponsored Head Start program at the Community Action Day School.* Bottom: *Salt River Indian School second grade making a space station.*

offer made by the white Virginians on the basis that white
education of Indian children left much to be desired in helping the latter to adjust to tribal life. In a letter rejecting the
offer, the spokesman for the Indians stated that the children
who had previously been educated in white institutions
returned to the tribes "bad runners, ignorant of every means
of living in the woods, unable to bear the cold or hunger;
they knew neither how to build a cabin, take a deer, or kill
an enemy; spoke our language imperfectly; were therefore
neither fit for hunters, warriors, or counselors; they were
totally good for nothing." The chiefs offered instead to handle
the education of a dozen white youths to "instruct them in
all we know, and make men of them."

Second only to the issue of relevancy has been the controversy centered around which institutional arrangement
is best suited for the education of Indian children. This issue
was first faced some 400 years ago by two monastic orders.
The first recorded formal attempt to educate Indians by the
white settlers dates back to 1568 when the Jesuits established a school for the instruction of Florida Indians. The
Indian children were transported to a Havana mission for
their education. In contrast to the Jesuits' attempt to educate
Indian children by removing them from their families, the
Franciscans gathered their followers into little villages and
taught them the skills they needed to make a better life for
themselves. Thus, the first encounters between the Indians
and the religious orders raised the question of whether it
is better to educate Indian children in their own environment
or to remove them to "better" surroundings.

Not to be outdone by the Catholic orders, the Protestant
settlers also attempted to "reach" the Indians by educating
their children. An early effort by John Eliot in the mid-seven-
teenth century established a series of schools for Indian children. The formal curriculum dictated that, in addition to
instructing the Indian children in letters, crafts, habits of

industry and thrift, and Christian ethics, they should also be taught Latin and Greek. Like their monastic counterparts, the Protestant ministers and educators also debated the relative virtues of educating the children within their communities or moving them from the Indian environment, by placing the children either in boarding schools or in the homes of settlers who would teach the natives the superior ways of the immigrants. But as every modern-day television viewer is aware, the story of interaction between the white settlers and the native Americans was not one of acculturation and accommodation. Attempts to assimilate the American Indian into the newly dominant culture of the white man were periodically interrupted by counterefforts of total exclusion or the ultimate solution of the "Indian problem" by their annihilation.

Apart from a few isolated acts of generosity—appropriating a few hundred dollars here and several thousand dollars somewhere else—the United States government did very little during the first century of the republic to educate Indian children. The armed forces, however, did help to lessen the magnitude of the problem by reducing the numbers of Indians who would have to be educated. Possibly the first step in present-day federal support of Indian education dates back to 1879 when the federal government funded an off-reservation boarding school in Carlisle, Pennsylvania. As envisioned by General Pratt, the founder of the Carlisle School, the boarding school was to provide a combination of academic and vocational training and thus help Indians adapt to the white civilization.

The establishment of the first federally supported Indian vocational school started a debate which persists to this day. Nearly half a century after the establishment of the Carlisle School, the Hoover administration commissioned the Institute of Government Research (later renamed The Brookings Institution) to study the federal government's administration of Indian affairs, including educational institutions. The result was the Meriam Report, which denounced boarding schools for their ineffective teaching methods, dilapidated housing facilities, staff cruelties to students, widespread malnutrition, and harsh disciplinary restrictions.[1] The reaction to the Meriam Report presumably spurred a deemphasis of the role of boarding schools and resulted in attempts to replace them with day schools and absorb some of the students into the public schools.

The trend during the past 30 or 40 years has been to expand Indian enrollment in regular public schools and shift the responsibility for the education of Indian children on reservations from the federal government to states and communities. But since Indians living on reservations are exempt from property taxes and contribute little to state or local taxes, the Johnson-O'Malley Act was passed in 1934 to provide for federal government reimbursement to states and localities enrolling Indian children in their schools. This law established the concept of federal support to public schools that are burdened by the enrollment of children resulting from federal activities. Two other laws enacted 16 years later expanded assistance to federally impacted states and communities encompassing school districts that enroll large numbers of Indian children. Public Law No. 81-815 provides for financial help for school construction, and Pub. L. No. 81-874 attempts to reimburse the school districts for the tax exemption of Indian lands in those areas that have experienced an increase in enrollment of reservation children.

Despite the expansion of federal assistance for Indian education during the 20 years since the three laws have been enacted, the majority of Indian children attending public schools are denied financial aid sufficient to cover the cost of their schooling. The Bureau of Indian Affairs estimates that a total of 178,000 Indian children living on or near Indian reservations attended school during the 1969–70 academic year. Two-thirds of these children attended public elementary and secondary schools, but total federal contributions to these schools under the Johnson-O'Malley Act and Pub. L. No. 81-874 amounted to only $31.9 million in 1970. No school construction under Pub. L. No. 81-815 was funded during that fiscal year. Mission schools, some dating to the colonial period, still enrolled about 6 of every 100 children attending school, but federal help to these schools was discontinued more than 50 years ago. The balance attended schools funded by the BIA.

More recently, Indian children have benefited from expanded government support for children from poverty-stricken homes. During academic year 1969–70, the federal government contributed a total of 160 million dollars for the education of Indian children (Table 8).

EARLY CHILDHOOD EDUCATION

Reservation children have been the beneficiaries of Head Start, possibly the most successful experimental program funded under the Great Society's antipoverty efforts. Designed to prepare preschool children for successful entry into elementary school, the concept is most appropriate for reservation children. The program emphasizes the academic growth of the child and attempts to incorporate the improvement of those aspects of child development that can normally be assumed by more affluent families. Head Start offers such extra scholastic benefits as medical, dental, and dietary assistance and parental involvement in community planning and administration.

Head Start is tailor-made for reservation toddlers and their families. The community participation aspect of Head Start programs is probably its most universally significant feature on Indian reservations. Instead of being directed from Wash-

Table 8. *Funds Allocated to Indian Education by Type of Program, 1969–70*

	AMOUNT (THOUSANDS)	NUMBER OF CHILDREN
Total	$198,499	°
Boarding schools	62,649	35,725
Day schools	15,304	17,160
Rough Rock Demonstration School	438	330
Institute of American Indian Arts	1,188	360
BIA dormitories	4,227	4,122
Scholarship grants	3,848	4,300
Administrative overhead	13,329	—
School construction and maintenance	38,200	—
Pub. L. No. 81-874 } Public	15,352	67,000
Johnson-O'Malley } school	16,542	
Elementary and Secondary Education Act — Title I (federal schools)	10,660	57,698
— Title I (Johnson-O'Malley public schools)	6,300	—
Pub. L. No. 89-329 — Title V-B Teacher Corps In-service Program	262	—
Head Start	10,200	10,000

° Not available because some children benefit from more than one program.
Source: Bureau of Indian Affairs and U.S. Office of Education.

ington or by the BIA area agents, Indians are being encouraged to plan and implement their own program for their own children. Community members are involved in every aspect of the project—from suggesting plans and funding proposals to administering the local projects, building the classrooms, and designing the curriculum. But possibly the most significant aspect of Head Start is that it serves as a prep school for Indian children to enter public schools. In addition to the usual impediments of children from poor homes, reservation children frequently enter school without any knowledge of

English. To help them prepare for public school education, Head Start exposes children on most reservations to bilingual experience and thus helps them prepare for public school education.

The multifaceted Head Start endeavor is costly. In addition to providing special services, Head Start emphasizes a high teacher-student ratio. Head Start guidelines dictate an optimum number of one professional teacher for every 15 children and the employment of subprofessionals and volunteers to relieve the workload of the teacher and provide additional attention for the child. As a result, $10.2 million allocated by Head Start to Indian reservations during fiscal 1970 was sufficient to provide for 10,000 children on 59 reservations, and most of these children were provided with year-round Head Start facilities.

Although skeptics continue to question the effectiveness of Head Start, its popularity cannot be denied, and the Bureau of Indian Affairs has indicated its enthusiasm for beginning the education of reservation children prior to the customary age of six. While the BIA had previously attempted to obtain funds for a preschool program, Congress waited for its cue from the success of the Head Start experience and finally voted to initiate kindergarten classes on reservations beginning in September 1968. BIA kindergarten activities are funded as a separately allocated appropriation, but they are based on the models developed by Head Start. Teacher aides are an essential component of both programs, and these aides are normally selected from the parents or other reservation adults able to speak both English and the native language of their tribe. During the school year 1968–69, 761 reservation children, 650 of whom were five-year-olds, attended Bureau of Indian Affairs kindergarten classes. An additional 2,400 five-year-olds attended public school kindergarten programs supported by Johnson-O'Malley funds from the BIA.

Preschool programs for Indian children are essentially a

compensatory program designed to ready these youngsters to enter regular schools. Both Head Start and the Bureau of Indian Affairs kindergarten programs are supplementary to conventional formal education. Not only have they brought attention to the difficulties Indian children have in the existing schools, but they have also illustrated possible approaches to the improvement and revision of the Indian educational system.

SCHOOLING

The availability of preschool facilities is a recent development and largely a product of new funding made available by the Great Society's programs. Changes in elementary and secondary schools have been much less dramatic (Table 9). A majority of Indian children living on or near reservations are enrolled in public schools, and the percentage of Indians attending public schools has not changed very much since the 1930s. Forty-one of every one hundred children and youths attended BIA schools in 1969 compared with 53 per-

Table 9. *Annual School Census of Indian Children, Age 6–18, 1939–1969*

	1939	1950	1959	1969*
Total population	86,668	103,073	144,069	198,965
Total in school	69,149	77,175	131,927	178,476
Public	36,558	36,090	81,098	119,123
Federal	25,525	32,657	38,911	48,789
Boarding	10,661	16,838	22,228	36,263 †
Day	14,268	15,570	16,683	16,100
Hospital	596	249	‡	108
Mission and other	7,066	8,428	11,918	10,564
Not in school	11,642	18,341	8,963	12,507
Definite information not available	5,877	7,557	3,179	7,982

* Ages 5–18.
†Figures do not add because federal breakdown includes children of all ages.
‡Not shown separately.
Source: Bureau of Indian Affairs.

cent three decades earlier. The relative importance of mission schools, on the other hand, has declined sharply. Before World War II, one of every nine Indian children attending school was in a mission school; according to latest available data, only 6 percent of the total are in mission schools.

In 1969 the BIA operated a total of 223 schools with a total enrollment of 52,471 children. An additional 4,089 children were provided dormitory facilities but attended public schools. The Navajo reservation claimed 48 of the 77 boarding schools, and of a total of 16,000 children enrolled in 144 day schools, 38 percent were Alaskan natives. Included as day schools were two hospital schools for children with long-term illnesses. Native Alaskans, Navajos, Sioux, and Pueblos together comprise 78 percent of the total federal enrollment.

Enrollment in boarding schools ranged from 2,100 in a modern facility in Utah to a small school accommodating some 40 children. The range of day school facilities is much smaller with enrollments varying from less than 20 children on smaller reservations to a large central school in Turtle Mountain, North Dakota, with more than 1,200 children (Table 10).

The Bureau of Indian Affairs' official policy is to encourage Indian children to attend public schools whenever it is at all feasible. If there is no public school within a commuting distance of the child's home, the Bureau claims to make every attempt for the children to attend a federal day school. In actuality, the proportion of federal students attending boarding schools has increased over the years. While only 42 percent of these children lived in boarding schools in 1939, 57 percent went to boarding schools in 1959 and 69 percent in 1969. Much of the increase in the boarding school enrollment during the 1950s was due to a successful campaign to extend educational opportunities to more Navajo children. Granted that those children living in isolated areas where there is

Table 10. *Boarding and Day Schools by Size of Enrollment, 1968–1969**

ENROLL-MENT	BOARDING † TOTAL EN-ROLL-MENT	NUMBER OF SCHOOLS	DAY TOTAL EN-ROLL-MENT	NUMBER OF SCHOOLS	COMBINATION TOTAL EN-ROLL-MENT	NUMBER OF SCHOOLS
Total	24,391	48	16,100	144	11,872	29
Less than 20	—	—	123	7	—	—
20–49	117	3	1,673	44	—	—
50–99	262	4	3,581	50	77	1
100–199	710	5	3,338	24	959	7
200–299	1,503	6	2,885	12	1,405	6
300–399	2,033	6	669	2	715	2
400–499	1,697	4	402	1	407	1
500–599	1,096	2	1,162	2	2,135	4
600–699	2,567	4	—	—	3,319	5
700–799	788	1	—	—	—	—
800–899	4,198	5	—	—	836	1
900–999	1,876	2	—	—	962	1
Over 1,000	7,554	6	2,237	2	1,057	1

* Two hospital schools with a total enrollment of 108 are not included.
† Four schools with a total of eight day students are included in this category.
Source: Bureau of Indian Affairs, computed from data in *Fiscal Year 1969 Statistics Concerning Education.*

no transportation available to enable them to enroll in a school within commuting distance must be sent to boarding schools, the statistics are evidence that the BIA is making no progress toward a reduction in the number of children who must go to school away from their own communities.

About 6,000 of those children enrolled in BIA day schools are native Eskimos or Aleuts. The Bureau has found that the distribution of the Alaskan population lends itself to the establishment of day schools instead of the unpopular boarding schools. This is due to the compact village arrangements in which the Eskimos and Aleuts live. Over 4,000 Indian children in the Aberdeen area, spanning North and South Dakota, and 2,000 in the Phoenix, Arizona, area attend day schools. Another 3,000 day school students are equally divided among the United Pueblos in Albuquerque, New Mexico; the Navajos; and the Cherokees. Attending boarding schools on a day basis are about 1,600 children in the Aberdeen area and 1,400 Navajo students.

The federal schools concentrate primarily upon the first few years of formal education. Of those attending a federal school, 44 percent are in the beginners through the fourth grades, and 3.8 percent of the students are in either ungraded elementary or secondary schools. As the proportionate enrollment of children in BIA schools has gradually been declining and the number of Indians going to public schools has been increasing, it is obvious that the Bureau's policy toward public school education is being heeded by parents and school administrators.

The curriculum of the federal day school is similar to that of most public schools throughout the nation and follows closely the curriculum in the surrounding public schools. While the Bureau of Indian Affairs professes to be in the process of revising its curriculum to better suit the needs of its Indian constituents, the children continue to receive "standard" formal education.

BOARDING SCHOOLS

The survival of the boarding school is a product of diverse interests and needs as well as bureaucratic perseverance. Few have many good words for the Indian boarding school system, and the schools have been attacked by students, parents, teachers, and even the Bureau of Indian Affairs. It is argued, nonetheless, that so long as many Indian tribes and families continue to live in isolation without adequate transportation and road facilities, there remains a need to provide boarding schools for Indian children if they are to be offered acceptable schooling facilities. Still there is little evidence that the BIA has made concerted efforts to place Indian children in regular public schools or to provide a school in all cases where such facilities would be feasible. Many parents apparently also find boarding schools a convenience; not that Indians love their children less than other groups, but the temptation to pack off beloved offspring to free boarding schools, as many wealthy parents can testify, is attractive. The facilities of BIA boarding schools cannot honestly be compared with private boarding schools, but in many cases the food and living facilities, spartan as they may be, are superior to the provisions that a poor Indian family may be able to afford for its children. So while few apparently like the boarding schools, some 35,000 Indian children from reservations are enrolled in 77 boarding schools operated by BIA, and their numbers have increased during the past decade despite all the attacks.

For purposes of an objective appraisal of the boarding school, one may disregard the official BIA pronouncement which suggested that the primary function of the boarding school is "to provide a well-rounded rich home experience as good as *any* child might have" (emphasis supplied). Equally unrepresentative are the horrendous stories promulgated by the public media about child beating and forced menial labor.

The fact is that the mission conferred upon boarding schools is very difficult and perhaps unattainable. Aside from attempting to educate and providing food and shelter, the typical boarding school deals not only with problems of communicating with children from a distinct culture, but frequently with serving in the same school children from more than one tribe who speak different languages and have different cultural backgrounds. The boarding school is basically an institution for handicapped Indian children. The child who lives in the school suffers from any one of a number of different hardships: he may come from a geographically isolated area; he may be several years overage for his grade achievement; he may be an orphan or a child of imprisoned, hospitalized, or separated parents; he may be criminally delinquent; or he may have been unable or unwilling to adapt to a day school and was transferred to the boarding school as a last resort.

Under the best of circumstances, the educators in the Indian boarding schools would have a very difficult task. Their problems have been compounded by their own lack of sensitivity to the values and culture of their wards. After nearly a century of experience, the BIA still has not developed the appropriate textbooks and materials to satisfy the special needs of Indian children in boarding schools. Efforts made during the 1930s to develop bilingual texts have been discarded and until recently have found little support among BIA officialdom. The BIA schools continue to teach Indian children that Columbus discovered America and that history on this continent began with the sixteenth century.

Aside from a questionable intellectual fare, minimal resources are allocated to the upkeep of boarding schools, and the low budget permits few, if any, "frills." As a rule, there is little planned recreation or counselors to help children in trouble or troubled children. Such "extras" require additional staff, and the BIA has not been very successful in securing the funds from Congress.

FUNDING

Assuming that expenditures were equally divided among all children attending federal schools, the total per capita expenditure during the 1969–70 school year was approximately $2,600. Altogether the BIA spent $1,769 per student enrolled in its boarding schools during the same year, compared with the average of $2,800 spent for each east coast private boarding school student (Table 11). Excluded from

Table 11. *Breakdown of Boarding School Cost per Child,*
1970 Estimate

	TOTAL (THOUSANDS)	PER CHILD†
Total	$63,837	$1,769.49
Enrollee expense	7,521	208.42
Travel	838	23.21
Clothing	33*	.92
Subsistence 1,655,804–Dormitory	6,561	181.81
4,905,012–Food		
Recreation	89	2.48
Materials	977	27.50
Texts	377	10.88
Audio-visual aids	30	.82
Supplies	503	13.94
Classroom furnishings	67	1.86
Operations and Maintenance	8,212	227.58
Personnel	47,127	1,305.99
Teachers	16,748	464.13
Administrative	2,580	71.49
Guidance	4,089	113.31
Aides (teacher)	130	3.60
Dormitory	12,250	339.48
Recreational	472	13.07
Bus driver	469	12.99
Food services	4,124	114.29
Library services	324	8.99
Clerical	345	9.55
Summer programs	324	8.98
Local school transportation	402	11.14
Other	4,870	134.97

* Clothing furnished by family or agency from which the child comes. BIA clothing fund
   only for emergencies.
† Based on an enrollment of 36,085.
Source: Bureau of Indian Affairs.

these costs are expenditures for medical and dental care,
which are provided by the Indian Health Service, and the
cost of constructing new facilities. The leanness of the BIA
budget is possibly best reflected in the fact that during the
school year an average of $2.48 per child was spent for the
students' recreation. The data also indicate that the BIA

was slow in adapting the use of the teacher aides encouraged under other federally subsidized educational programs. While the Bureau professes to have been interested in aides for decades, the actual level of funding belies any such good intentions. The use of teacher aides could have been particularly beneficial in Bureau schools if the funds were used to employ Indians who might have established a better rapport with the children. And of course the BIA outlays do not cover all the children's needs. Only $.92 was spent per child for clothing. Clothes worn by children in BIA schools had to be provided by their tribes or their families. It is not unusual for a child attending a BIA school to possess only a minimal clothing change and one pair of shoes.

Despite the very lean budget provided for boarding schools, there are 40,000 children (including 4,100 living in BIA dormitories but attending public schools) living in federal schools. These schools accounted for more than half of total federal expenditures for the education of Indian children living on or near reservations.

The budget for day schools in 1970 was a relatively generous one of $891 for each student ($15.3 million divided by 17,160 children). This amount was 24 percent higher than the national average of $717 per child. The higher costs are understandable. The BIA reservations tend to enroll a small number of children, and a wide dispersion of these schools prevents economies of size. The total school expenditure is necessarily raised by the day school service of offering their pupils a morning snack and a warm lunch.

PUBLIC SCHOOLS

In addition to maintaining boarding and day schools for Indian children, the federal government contributes to the education of Indian students attending public schools. During academic year 1968–69 a total of 119,123 Indian children between the ages of 6 and 18 living on or near reservations attended public schools, and in fiscal 1970 the federal government contributed a total of $31.9 million to state and local educational systems to defray part of the cost of educating Indian children. Not all school districts enrolling Indian children received help, and even those schools that did obtain assistance were reimbursed for only part of their investment in Indian children. Based on the 1969 enrollment, the federal government invested an average of $268 per Indian child under legislation specifically aimed for the purpose of assisting the public schools with heavy Indian enrollments. In addition, the federal government contributed more than $17 million for the education of Indian children in both BIA and public schools under the Elementary and Secondary Education Act, which is largely aimed at helping school districts with a high concentration of children from poor homes. Most reservation families qualify for this type of help by virtue of their low income.

The Johnson-O'Malley Act provided $16.5 million in 1969–70 with which the BIA made grants to public schools educating Indian children. Pub. L. No. 81-874 reimbursed school districts $15.4 million in fiscal 1970 in lieu of taxes in those areas where the enrollment of Indian students expanded public school populations.

EDUCATIONAL PERSONNEL

Teachers in BIA schools, like other BIA employees, are federal civil service employees and subject to federal pay regulations. Federal classification regulations are quite rigid, and all BIA teachers are slotted in the salary schedule. Based on 1970 federal salary schedules, a teacher's beginning annual salary was $8,100, and a teacher with 5 years' experience normally received $9,200. These rates were more than competitive with salaries of public school teachers in states with a high Indian concentration. Nonetheless, like most rural schools, BIA schools have experienced serious problems of teacher turnover. Statistics are not very conclusive, but available data seem to indicate that the annual teacher turnover is 25 percent, somewhat higher than turnover in schools adjacent to reservations.

Only about one of every six reservation teachers is Indian. The low proportion of Indian teachers is not due to BIA discrimination, but rather to the unavailability of teachers who qualify under the civil service regulations. Whether these qualification requirements are relevant or serve the Indian children well is a crucial question which the BIA has not attempted to discern through experimentation or alterations in required credentials. A major shortcoming of the white teachers working in BIA schools is their ignorance of Indian culture.

As the schools attended by Indian students are generally administered and staffed by whites, it is no wonder that they are oriented to values and behavioral patterns that are foreign to the students. The cultural conflict is magnified, moreover, when the teachers themselves are oblivious to the differences which the Indian youngsters must overcome to become effectively integrated into the school environment. Such concrete and visible differences as dress, language, and hairstyles are rarely unobserved, but the more significant factors of attitudes, mores, and sentiments are often overlooked. While some have documented a lack of knowledge of Indian ways on the part of the teachers, others have noticed a general lack of sensitivity, of empathy toward the problems the Indian must face in the academic atmosphere. The most common reason for this lack of awareness of the intangible aspects of the Indian student's world is not lack of interest or desire to know the students, as one might expect, but a mere lack of contact with Indians. Many teachers come to the reservation only between the hours of 9 and 3, reside in all-white areas, and have little interaction with the Indian community they serve. If motivation, psychological readiness, and healthy attitudes are essential for education, then sensitivity to the Indian child is a necessary qualification for his teacher.

HIGHER EDUCATION

Compared with national norms, few reservation Indians enroll in colleges, and of those who enter college, only a very small proportion graduate. It might be more appropriate to compare Indian college attendance with college enrollment of youths from poverty-stricken homes. On that basis, the record of Indians is rather favorable. The proportion of Indians attending college has been increasing; while in 1936, only 1 of every 15 Indian high school graduates went to college, the number increased to 1 of every 6 in 1950,[2] and according to the latest information, 28.8 percent of Indian federal high school graduates entered college.[3]

No less serious than the relatively low number of Indians who enter an institution of higher learning is the high drop-out rate of those who are admitted for a college education. Factors contributing to the high drop-out rate are complex and include difficulties relating to academic, personal, and social adjustment. For example, a study of 100 Indians enrolled in the University of New Mexico found that 70 percent dropped out because of poor grades (the drop-out rate for all other students was 49 percent), and even the majority of the 30 percent of Indians who remained in school had been placed on academic probation at one time or another.[4]

While the inordinate drop-out rate of Indians from college has been well documented, pinpointing the causes is much more difficult. Obviously, cultural impediments are significant. Apparently, Indians do not ascribe the same importance to "getting ahead" as the white population. It has been found that Indians who hold most tightly to the traditional tribal culture have the most difficulty adjusting to a college environment, especially when tribal values conflict with the ethic of competition.[5] Proficiency in English remains a problem for the Indian college student as it was in his earlier school years.

Whatever the obstacles to entering college and pursuing his course of study, the availability of basic support for an Indian youth is not a major problem. Indian students are eligible to receive federal assistance from the liberally expanded National Defense Education Act of 1958. Most Indian youths are also eligible for aid under the various antipoverty programs enacted in the 1960s. In addition, the BIA maintains a scholarship fund which in academic year 1969–70 amounted to $3,848,000 used to support 4,300 students attending school. Several tribes also maintain their own scholarship funds. During the school year 1969–70, 1,400 college students from 40 different reservations were assisted by their tribal college funds. From a total of $1.1 million in tribal scholarships, loans, and grants awarded, the amount of assistance per student ranged from $43 to $8,333 and averaged about $809, indicating that in most cases tribal assistance was supplementary to other support available to Indian students.

A major contributing factor to the Indian's difficulty in achieving success in college is the lack of counseling available to Indian high school students who are capable of pursuing a college education. Part of this gap is being filled by Upward Bound, a program initiated under the Economic Opportunity Act and concentrated upon motivating poor youths to enter college. Private organizations have complemented the work of Upward Bound and have offered both counseling and scholarships to Indian students. The best known of these organizations is the United Scholarship Service, a national, private, nonprofit corporation in Denver which provides financial aid for American Indians and Mexican-American students. In addition to providing grants, this service refers students to other agencies that may be able to assist them.

Despite the multiplicity of sources, many Indian students are not "reached" by the programs. BIA grants are largely restricted to students whose families are enrolled in a federally recognized tribe and who are one-quarter Indian blood. The grants also try to single out students with the highest academic achievements, thus excluding many Indian youths who have the potential to benefit from a college education. Also excluded from eligibility for most scholarships are married students and those enrolled in graduate programs. A realistic scholarship program for Indian youths would take into consideration the special needs of Indian students and would establish criteria applicable to individual abilities and Indian community needs.

AN ASSESSMENT

On a per capita basis, the American society spends more resources educating Indian children than other groups. Nonetheless, an examination of Indian educational achievements does not reflect the added expenditures. But comparisons may not be applicable, since Indian children face even greater obstacles to obtaining an education than other minority groups. Experts may disagree upon the impact of other presumed subcultures of poverty; there can be, however, little disagreement that Indian children come from a totally different culture and that educational and other institutions adapted for the needs of the dominant society in the United States may not be appropriate for Indians.

Still, in order to "make it" in contemporary American society, Indian children must achieve the same educational levels as the majority. Prejudice and discrimination may prevent an Indian from receiving an equal break even when he achieves a competitive status.

Available data indicate that Indians do receive an inferior education either because they are poor achievers in school or because the schools fail them. According to the 1960 census, adult Indians completed 8.4 years of education compared with 10.9 years for whites and 8.2 years for blacks. For the crucial young-adult population 14–24 years of age, the average number of years completed by Indians was 9.0 as compared with 10.8 for the general population. The disadvantaged position of Indian youth is more pronounced when comparisons are made on the basis of actual educational achievement rather than years of school attended, for Indians generally do not perform up to their grade level. While many studies find no significant difference between the achievement levels of Indian and non-Indian students in the first three years of school, the vast majority report that Indian academic performance declines as the students advance through the grades. One study found that the educational retardation among the Indian student population is 7 months in the third grade, 14 months in the fifth grade, and 15 months in the sixth grade. The cause of this effect has not been determined, but such contributing factors as language difficulties, psychological alienation, the ability to deal with the quantitative comprehension, and impoverished background have been linked with the retardation.[6] However, when culture biases are eliminated on non-verbal tests, Indian children performed as well as white students.[7] Standardized achievement tests measure, at best, how "white" the Indian is. To make the educational system more relevant (to use an overworked, but nevertheless appropriate term) to the Indian child, it will be necessary to adapt the system to measure educational achievement by standards appropriate for the Indian community.

Alleged lack of interest and "negative" attitudes of Indians toward education may be more a reflection of lack of relevancy than of hostility. The Indian parent may find that educational achievement would encourage the child to seek his fortune in the white man's ways and forsake reservation life.

With the moving of industry and technology on or near reservations and the gradual decline of racial discrimination in American economic life, conventional American education is becoming increasingly relevant to life on the reservation. Some parents, and sometimes whole tribes, want their children to attend public schools to become integrated into the more lucrative dominant society, and others stress education to gain a comparative advantage in competition with the whites. Many times the favorable attitude toward education is strictly pragmatic—to secure a better job, to obtain more material goods, to learn to speak English to better understand commercial media. Even if a tribe has a basic distrust of the Anglos, it wants the government to provide its children with better educational facilities.

Caution must be exercised to avoid lumping all Indians into any one attitudinal bag. They do not, contrary to most stereotyped images, think or behave as a homogeneous mass. Some Indians place a high value on knowledge for knowledge's sake; some make an effort to acquire the skills and abilities American education offers them; and some even become absorbed into the general society and are culturally undistinguished from other American groups. But there remain still more who want to maintain their Indian identity or who stress the ideology of Red Power and positive segregation. It is obvious that all these orientations affect the Indian attitude toward education and that parental values will influence the student's. The American Indian education system must learn to deal effectively with these variations.

Low achievement levels, high drop-out rates, and conflicting attitudes toward education are by no means the only problems faced by the Indian student. He has other emotional and social problems which are unique to red people, and he shares many of the difficulties of minority groups in any locale. Some of the special problems of the Indian in the educational system stem from cultural differentiation, culture conflicts, and language difficulties.

The accumulated cultural knowledge of the young Indian is often not of the sort required for success in existing school programs. The children are simply unfamiliar with many of the concepts and objects which teachers assume are general knowledge acquired by all children before they enter the first grade. While young Indians may have an intimate knowledge of animals, the land, mythology, and the abstract nuances of their religion, they find the "Dick and Jane" curriculum of the elementary school strange and unintelligible. The many positive values of Indian heritage should be recognized and utilized in the classroom to make learning a pleasurable and functional process.

Certainly the Indian child begins school with a different cultural background than is generally expected by school administrators, teachers, and planners. This background, while always distinct from that of a white child, varies from tribe to tribe and from child to child. Indian societies maintain the traditional values of the past to varying degrees, and traditional values in one tribe often bear no resemblance to those of another tribe.

While Indians have accepted, either voluntarily or through coercion, many of the material artifacts of the dominant society, such as television, automobiles, a money economy, and clothing styles, many persist in retaining the more abstract aspects of their old way of life. They still speak the tribal language, conceive of themselves as a separate people, and interact according to their own social patterns. The American Indian experience is not unique in that all societies are constantly undergoing processes of adaptation, adjustment, and accommodation to changing conditions. It is, therefore, not at all unusual that the Indian population should become assimilated into some spheres of American life while maintaining a distinct identity of "Indianness" in others.

The implications for education are obvious. All those concerned with the formal education of the Indian student must be aware of the cultural nuances of each child's background. Each school must be designed with an understanding and knowledge of the particular tribes it serves and each teacher must consider the customs, beliefs, and values of the children in his classroom when planning lessons, teaching concepts, or taking disciplinary action. Very few educators have dealt constructively with the problems arising from the conflict between the culture base of the school and that of the Indian student.

SELF-DETERMINATION

One obvious approach to achieve better accommodation between Indian education and their society is to give Indians greater control over their educational system. Control over their educational establishment is not going to resolve problems of malnutrition, impediments due to lack of medical attention, and other obstacles that stand in the way of many Indian children trying to achieve a sound education in accord with their own cultural values. Nonetheless, Indian control over their own schools would presumably ameliorate the conflicts between their schools and society and might also improve classroom instruction.

Offering American Indians opportunity to assume greater control over their schools is not new. In the 1930s and 1940s some community-centered schools encouraged parental participation in tribal education committees, Parent-Teacher Associations, and various afterschool and summer programs.

The Bureau of Indian Affairs adopted an official policy in 1951 that provided for an increase in community involvement in the selection of Indian school boards to serve in a purely advisory capacity to local school programs, and in 1967 a 16-member National Indian Education Advisory Committee was established to coordinate activities of the tribes with the Bureau. Finally, in 1968 President Johnson stated, "To help make the Indian school a vital part of the Indian community, I am directing the Secretary of the Interior to establish Indian school boards for Federal Indian schools. School board members—selected by their communities—will receive whatever training is necessary to enable them to carry out their responsibilities."[8]

And President Nixon voiced similar concerns in 1970 when he stated,

> We believe every Indian community wishing to do so should be able to control its own Indian schools. This control would be exercised by school boards selected by Indians and functioning much like other school boards throughout the nation. To assure that this goal is achieved, I am asking the Vice President, acting in his role as Chairman of the National Council on Indian Opportunity, to establish a Special Education Subcommittee of that Council.[9]

To implement President Johnson's rhetoric, the BIA announced the establishment of Project Tribe, designed to encourage involvement and active participation at all levels of school operation and aim ultimately for a system of public schools controlled and supported by Indians. The BIA, however, has not achieved a reputation for moving with lightning or even deliberate speed, and by the end of 1970, more than two years after the President's announcement, only four schools (The Ramah Navajo Community School of New Mexico, Stephan High School in South Dakota, and the Rough Rock and Blackwater schools in Arizona, enrolling a total of 950 students) were turned over by the BIA to tribal control. Although initial attempts to encourage tribes to take over the administration of their own schools met with little response, there is increasing interest among Indians in the formation of school boards. BIA officials deny any procrastination in carrying out the objectives of Project Tribe and insist that tribal councils refused to assume the responsibility for administering their own schools. The explanation is that tribal reluctance to accept a greater measure of self-determination is based on Indian fears that control over their own institutions would also be accompanied by termination of federal responsibilities toward reservations and the severing of federal assistance.

DEMONSTRATION SCHOOLS

Failing in initial efforts to turn over control of the schools to tribal councils, the BIA has funded the establishment of demonstration schools. Teaching English as a Second Language programs are being tested at a BIA School in Rock Point, and another school in New Mexico is preparing teachers for bilingual schools. Community-controlled schools include Stephan High School, Ramah High School, and the Blackwater School. The two demonstration schools that have received the most publicity are the Rough Rock Demonstration School and the Institute for American Indian Arts. Possibly the most significant single educational project has been the establishment of an all Indian College, the Navajo Community College.

The forerunner of the Rough Rock Demonstration School was initially funded by the Office of Economic Opportunity in 1965 at the BIA School in Lukachukai, Arizona. The original purpose was to turn over a BIA school to community control and to overhaul the school curriculum according to the wishes of the locally selected school board. The new board could not, however, take control because the Rough Rock school retained BIA staff and administrators. Since BIA schools adhere to civil service employment regulations, the school board found it could neither hire nor fire staff. Therefore, a nonprofit, private corporation of Navajo leaders was created to provide for a more flexible operation. The acronym for the new demonstration in Navajo Education (DINE) is also the Navajo word for The People.

The Board of Directors for DINE, composed of three prominent Navajo leaders, decided to accept BIA's offer of a new $3 million school at Rough Rock which had no ready-made staff. The Board of Directors and the Rough Rock community unanimously endorsed the school and took over control on July 1, 1966. Seven school board members were subsequently selected by the residents in a 15-mile radius affected by the school.

Despite the alleged disfavor of boarding schools, the new management of Rough Rock continued to maintain boarding facilities while transporting children whenever possible. But because of long distances and poor road conditions, more than half of the enrollees live in dormitories. The Rough Rock school, however, tried to put its own stamp on the boarding facilities and to adapt living conditions simulating a home environment. Four mothers reside in the girls' dorm, and four fathers and one mother live in the boys' dorm on a rotating basis.[10] The parents are paid a small stipend during the period they live in the dormitories.

The academic curriculum of the Rough Rock Demonstration School attempts to expose the children to *both* Navajo culture and subjects taught in public schools. Reading, writing, and speech are taught in both Navajo and English, and staff members are encouraged to use both languages interchangeably.

A Navajo Curriculum Center, funded partially by an Elementary and Secondary Education Act grant, is responsible for producing instructional materials for the school that deal with Navajo biographies, legends, history, and modern problems and programs. Several textbooks have already been published, and other supplementary items are being prepared. Information for the books is supplied by medicine men, storytellers, and community leaders; and a Navajo speaker, an English-speaking writer, two Navajo artists, an editor, a publisher, and an audio-visual specialist formally prepare the publications. Teachers serve as advisors and assistants with the projects.

A basic goal of the school is to secure community involvement. To encourage community interest, the school authorities encourage the school personnel to engage in various activities normally not considered part of a school's curriculum. Projects include the development of a small-scale cottage industry based on the school's arts and crafts program that provides training to 36 people a year. School resources are also being utilized to help people in the community manage their livestock and improve their agricultural production.

The experience of Rough Rock indicates the potential for change that can be brought about by utilizing school resources. In a community where organized community institutions are minimal, Rough Rock suggests that the school can play an increasing role in organizing community activities. Rough Rock further confirms the experience of many antipoverty educational projects which have been successful in utilizing services of parents and other nonprofessional personnel in performing useful functions in the school. It does not follow, however, that the experience of Rough Rock can be replicated in many other Indian communities. Since the cost of educating each student was $2,422 in 1970, it would require an expansion of BIA educational funds to duplicate the Rough Rock experience in other Indian communities, and more than funds is involved. Because of the sustained publicity the project received, Rough Rock attracted more than its share of VISTA volunteers, bilingual teachers, and other specialized personnel. Some of the talent utilized in Rough Rock is in short supply and cannot be easily duplicated in many other schools. The experience of Rough Rock does, however, suggest that the detailed control which BIA exercises over local schools is unnecessary and harmful and that local talent is available to administer schools. Since thousands of other American communities have already had that experience, the need for a demonstration project to prove what is self-evident appears to be of questionable value.

An entirely different type of demonstration school is the Institute of American Indian Arts. Founded in 1962, the school enrolls 350 students from 80 different tribes ranging from Alaska to Florida. The Institute is an accredited high school, but in addition to his regular academic subjects, each student is encouraged to study the artistic heritage of his own tribe and to select a major field of art in which to concentrate. The school has had a very high retention rate, and one of every three graduates has entered universities or college level art schools, a college entry rate much higher than that of other Indian high schools. Advocates of the Institute have been quick to conclude that the excellent academic record of the school has been due to the fact that students have been offered "meaningful" and "relevant" education. There appears to be little question about that aspect of the school activities. The students have won many art awards, performed in musical shows throughout the country, and participated in several major art shows and exhibitions. The success of the school may be due to the selectivity of students and the better-than-average support it receives from the BIA, but the experience of the school does suggest the need for diversifying the educational options available to Indian youth.

One way to replicate the successes of the Institute of American Indian Arts is to transform the BIA off-reservation boarding schools into specialized secondary institutions. Each of the schools could then devote its resources to the development of its own area of concentration, be it business education, industrial arts, college preparatory, fine arts, or other relevant specializations. Indian students, with the assistance of guidance counselors, would be able to select the school best suited to their interests, abilities, and career plans.

Possibly the most significant Indian education development in recent years has been the opening of the Navajo Community College, the first and only institution of higher learning administered and intended for American Indians. Located on the sprawling Navajo reservation, the new college opened in 1969 with an enrollment of more than 300 students, mostly Navajos. Reflecting the college's policy of open admission to all comers regardless of prior educational attainment, the student body is anything but typical, ranging from 17-year-old fully qualified students, to middle-aged women who speak only Navajo, to unemployed fathers with less than an elementary-grade education. If plans for the college materialize, its enrollment will rise to 1,500 before its tenth anniversary. A major function of the Navajo junior college is to prepare students for matriculation in an accredited college or university. Considering the wide diversity in student preparation, the college allows each student to progress at his own pace. It is hoped that some of the motivational and attitudinal problems encountered by Indian students in other colleges will be alleviated in this reduced-pressure atmosphere.

Traditional subjects are only one aspect of the Navajo Community College activities. Since many of the new enrollees speak only Navajo, English is taught as a second language, and the school offers vocational technical courses, including auto mechanics, secretarial training, and small business management.

LESSONS LEARNED AND FUTURE DIRECTION

Like most other educational establishments, the BIA officials responsible for the administration of programs to educate Indian children on or near reservations have not displayed great enthusiasm for change. Working within an entrenched bureaucracy, BIA's educational authorities continue to fund programs which may have been suitable in a different age and century. Reliance upon a reorganization of the Bureau, however, is too facile a solution to the problems of Indian education. But so long as the various layers of bureaucracy are retained and the Assistant Commissioner for Education has less power than the area directors, changes in the federal school system will be difficult to achieve. Experts have suggested that the function of education be made independent of the area directors, who are generally not educators and have little knowledge and specialized interest in the process of educating the young. Local field administrators would be directly accountable to the Assistant Commissioner who would have full responsibility for the entire program of education, thus eliminating an unnecessary and often restricting step in the present bureaucratic arrangement.

Likewise, the Indian clients of the BIA education program have been either apathetic or unable to force the BIA to redistribute the resources devoted to education and adapt the educational system to the needs and aspirations of Indian people. Repeated promises to make tribal representatives participants in the administration of schools for Indian children have not been fulfilled even though various demonstration projects have indicated Indian interest in revamping the educational institutions and their capability to achieve this end. There is also little evidence that the BIA has made serious efforts to reallocate available funds in order to achieve optimal results, and enrollment in the much criticized boarding schools remained unchanged over the past decade.

It would be misleading, however, to blame the shortcomings of Indian education solely on the BIA. There is little evidence that Indian tribal councils or other spokesmen for reservation Indians are clamoring to take over responsibility for administering the educational institutions. Nonetheless, the case for turning over the responsibility for educating Indian children to duly selected representatives from the reservations or nearby communities is persuasive. This goal will only be achieved if Congress takes direct action and provides for the machinery of passing federal funds for education directly to the Indian communities. Without congressional action, it is unlikely that the bureaucracy will voluntarily surrender its power. And so long as Congress insists upon earmarking funds, the federal bureaucracy cannot relinquish its power over the expenditures of these funds.

NOTES

1. Lewis Meriam et al., *Problems of Indian Administration,* The Johns Hopkins Press, Baltimore, 1928, pp. 392ff.

2. Robert J. Havighurst, "Education Among American Indians: Individual and Cultural Aspects," *Annals of the American Academy of Political and Social Science,* May, 1957, p. 114.

3. Bureau of Indian Affairs, "Summer Placement Report on Graduates, School Year 1968–69," unpublished document, Mar. 16, 1970.

4. Miles V. Zintz, *Education Across Cultures,* William C. Brown Book Company, Dubuque, Iowa, 1963, pp. 116–117.

5. Havighurst, loc. cit.

6. Miles V. Zintz, *The Indian Research Study: The Adjustment of Indian and Non-Indian Children in the Public Schools of New Mexico,* College of Education, The University of New Mexico, Albuquerque, 1960, p. 82.

7. Robert J. Havighurst and Rhea R. Hilkevitch, "The Intelligence of Indian Chil-

dren as Measured by a Performance Scale," *Journal of Abnormal and Social Psychology,* October 1944, pp. 419–433.

8. U.S. Department of the Interior, *Position Paper Concerning the Implications of Project Tribe (Indian School Boards),* Issue Support Paper No. 70-7, Fiscal Year 1970, Oct. 17, 1968, p. 8.

9. "The American Indians—Message From the President of the United States," *Congressional Record,* daily ed., July 8, 1970, p. H6440.

10. "Rough Rock Demonstration School," *Congressional Record,* daily ed., June 18, 1969, p. S6665.

"ALL THE THINGS THAT HAVE HARMED ME,
   THEY WILL LEAVE ME.
I WALK WITH A COOL BODY AFTER THEY LEAVE ME.
INSIDE OF ME TODAY I WILL BE WELL,
   ALL FEVER WILL HAVE COME OUT OF ME,
   AND GO AWAY FROM ME,
   AND LEAVE MY HEAD COOL."—NAVAJO BEAUTYWAY CHANT

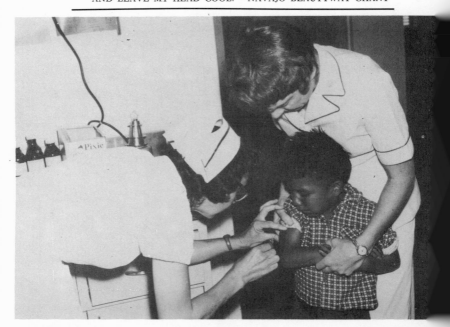

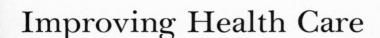

Chapter 3

Improving Health Care

INDIAN HEALTH SERVICE RESPONSIBILITIES

Unlike the Bureau of Indian Affairs, which assumes responsibility for the education of Indian children only when public facilities are not available on or near the reservation, the Indian Health Service of the Department of Health, Education, and Welfare has almost exclusive responsibility for the health care of the nation's reservation population. Whereas federal education programs for Indians are supplementary to those services for which Indians are eligible by virtue of their American citizenship, the health programs of the IHS, while intended to be residual, are generally the only services available for reservation residents.

The policy of the Indian Health Service is first to identify the health needs of the Indian population through the vital statistics available from the states in which Indians reside and through its own collection and assessment of pertinent data. An inventory of the resources available to help satisfy the assessed needs considers both the capacity of the IHS direct health care facilities and the services available to all citizens. When neither of these two sources can meet the

Top: *Navajo Indians creating a ritual sand painting for medicinal purposes.* Bottom: *Indian child receives medical assistance from Public Health Service personnel.*

needs of the people and when sufficient funds are available, the IHS purchases the services of private hospitals and medical practitioners. Because public and private facilities are simply unavailable on or near many reservations, the Indian Health Service nearly always relies upon its own direct services to provide health care for American Indians.

Officials of the Indian Health Service recognize, however, that IHS services consitute only one of several *potential* health resources and that federal appropriations will never be adequate for the IHS to be the sole source of medical attention. Realizing this fact and its position as primary caretaker of the health of American Indians, the IHS is increasingly emphasizing its advocacy role for the Indian people. This advocacy manifests itself in the various efforts the Indian Health Service has been undertaking to encourage federal, state, local, and private health-related agencies to provide health services for reservation Indians. For instance, when comprehensive health programs were being planned, states were required to establish a planning council, and the IHS encouraged Indians and its own staff to become active members of the various councils. It has been trying to encourage more Indian participation in entry-level training in the health professions. IHS staff members also work with the Indian people to provide encouragement and training to enable them to become their own advocates of increased and improved health care services.

One of the reasons the Indian health care program has nearly complete responsibility for the health of Indian people is that early treaty agreements made federally supported health services available for Indians before they were extended to other poor people. Once the programs were established, they continued under their own inertia with regular and generous congressional funding. So facilities for Indians were already in existence when such new federal programs as Medicare and Medicaid were created. Actually, few Indians benefit from Medicare and Medicaid. Thirty-six percent of the total Indian reservation population are in Arizona and Alaska where no Medicaid program is available; and in those states where Indians are eligible for Medicaid, coverage tends to be minimal. It may not be an accident that Alaska and Arizona have not adopted Medicaid, since the federal government now supplies all health outlays under IHS for their large Indian populations. It is estimated that only $3.5 million was expended in fiscal 1970 for both Medicare and Medicaid for Indians. The IHS often pays the deductible of this amount when no other program supplies the payment and frequently supplies the supplements when Medicare and Medicaid funds become exhausted. Despite the current lack of support by other federal health programs, the IHS continues to encourage eligible Indian people to register for Medicare, Medicaid, and Social Security.

HEALTH PROBLEMS

An Indian tends to view health as harmony with nature. To him, illness can be mental anguish, misfortune, family discord, physical pain, or any other sign of imbalance in the prescribed order and functioning of human existence. Certainly broader in scope than the traditional medical view of health as the absence of disease, this definition recognizes the integral relationships of mental, social, and physical health. There is a direct relationship between the levels of employment, education, housing, transportation, sanitation, nutrition, and economic development with the health of a people. It has long been recognized that a person without the resources to obtain adequate housing, a nutritional diet, a steady job, and a high level of education will also tend to be physically unhealthy.

SPECIAL MEDICAL PROBLEMS

Indians, Aleuts, and Eskimos are subject to higher incidence rates of certain illnesses that affect other Americans, and these illnesses are generally more severe and of longer duration among Indians than among most other population groups in the country. Even some diseases which occur so rarely among the rest of the United States population as to be virtually extinct strike the people of the reservation with frequency and severity. The Indian state of health is comparable to that of the United States population as a whole two or three generations ago, and Indian morbidity is generally caused by those diseases which were the primary sources of death for the total population in 1900.

The major health problems of Alaskan natives and American Indians, in order of both frequency and severity of occurrence, are: communicable diseases among children, accidents, mental health (including alcoholism), nutritional deficiencies, and dental deficiencies. It might be noted that the greatest single cause of death is accidents, many of which may be disguised suicides.[1] The prevalence of influenza, pneumonia and other respiratory diseases, gastroenteric conditions, streptococcal sore throats, and communicable diseases is higher among Indian children than among the general population. Incidences of streptococcal infections are eight to ten times higher; mortality from influenza and pneumonia is twice as high; and the death rate from tuberculosis is eight times greater.[2]

Although accurate data concerning the prevalence of malnutrition are not available, it is one of the most serious problems affecting Indian children. Cases of marasmus and kwashiorkor, the most severe forms of protein-calorie malnutrition, are too common among young reservation children. One study of all children under five years of age admitted to the Tuba City Public Health Hospital in Arizona revealed that of a total of 5,430 admittals, 116 had a diagnosis of malnutrition, 27 of whom had marasmus and 17 of whom suffered from kwashiorkor.[3] Besides being dehabilitating itself, malnutrition is a direct cause of the Indian's susceptibility to disease.

It is estimated that mental health problems are two or three times higher among Indians, suicides fifteen percent higher, and alcoholism and glue, paint, and gasoline sniffing considerably more prevalent among Indians than among the rest of the population.[4] Mental health difficulties are especially prevalent among young Indians. Suicides, for example, are more common for Indian youth than for the general population, but they are less common among Indian adults than among adults in the rest of the population. Trachoma, a contagious and potentially blinding eye infliction, is extremely common on the Indian reservations of the Southwest. While cases of tuberculosis have declined steadily, the disease still strikes Indians eight times more frequently than other Americans. It appears that the Indian is plagued by more diseases and more severe symptoms of these illnesses than other groups in the country.

Two unique facets of the Indian health situation deserve mention. First, it has been noted that different tribal groups suffer more from different types of illnesses. Congenital hip dislocations are common among Apaches and Navajos, and congenital heart disease is almost three times more evident in Apaches than in the rest of the nation. Microbial infections cause three-fourths of the sicknesses of tradition-oriented Navajo Indians, while the more assimilated Oklahoma Indians are more often victims of obesity, hypertension, and diabetes (all associated with modern middle-class society). Alaskan children are particularly prone to bronchiectasis (destruction of air passages) and otitis media (infection of the middle ear). Bronchiectasis strikes children as early as five months after they are born and is usually a totally disabling disease. It is thought that there may be a direct connection between inhalation of seal oil during feeding and an incidence rate of bronchiectasis that is over 40 times greater than for the rest of the United States. Middle ear infections, while high generally among Indian groups, are treated at the rate of about 12,000 per year in the Alaskan native health area. Running ears are said to be as common among little Alaskans as running noses are among children of middle-class suburbia.[5]

The second unique and significant fact about Indian health is that so many diseases strike the very young. Pediatric patients account for over one-third of the total admissions to Public Health hospitals, a rate which is three times higher than for the rest of the country. As great a percentage of deaths occur among Indian children under age 1 as among those under 45 for the rest of the population. The death rate from gastroenteritis among children under five is about eight times greater, and death rates from respiratory, digestive, and infective diseases, accidents, and congenital malformations are all significantly higher among Indian children.[6]

ENVIRONMENTAL PROBLEMS

Health is neither a purely individual nor strictly physical condition. The social, economic, and environmental conditions on reservations are conducive to poor health and problematic to the provision of health services and the consequent attainment of better health. Substandard housing, geographic isolation, poverty, primitive transportation, and a lack of adequate communication systems all concretely contribute to the health problem and the difficulty of its resolution. Cultural conflict in the form of health traditions, value systems, and religious practices are major factors in the challenge to the Indian Health Service medical personnel to provide the benefits of "white medicine" on the reservation.

Housing facilities on reservations are almost universally inadequate and conducive to poor health. Over half the Indian and Alaskan native families live in self-made one- or two-room homes constructed from whatever materials are freely available on the land and are generally unsuited to severe climatic conditions. Usually five or six persons crowd into these dwelling units.

The heating systems often consist of fireplaces or wood-burning stoves that are used for both warmth and cooking. Most dwelling units have no water source on the premises, so water (which is frequently contaminated) is hauled over long distances from creeks, wells, and sink holes. Over half of the Indian homes have no indoor bathrooms, and 45 percent of the outdoor privies and sewage-disposal facilities have been judged totally inadequate by sanitation experts. Rarely is there any acceptable method of refuse disposal; pest control is virtually absent; and food sanitation practices are usually unsatisfactory.[7]

Isolation is of vital concern to those interested in the health care of our Indian population. Especially acute on the Navajo reservation and in Alaska, geographic isolation is compounded by a lack of adequate transportation facilities. Those in need of medical attention must travel up to hundreds of miles over primitive roads and rough terrain, often by foot or in a borrowed car. Ambulance and air transportation are inadequate even in those few areas where they are available. Ambulance service is only provided within a 70- to 90-mile radius, and many families must travel long distances to reach a road over which a motor vehicle can travel. And there are few Indians who have telephones to call for emergency service. While public health officials do visit isolated areas on a regular basis, there is no guarantee that acute or emergency cases can wait to see a medical worker on his appointed days. Consequently, there are innumerable instances of lives that could have been saved had decent transportation to hospitals been available.

The single most direct cause of the many environmental factors affecting ill health among American Indians is poverty. They simply cannot afford to provide themselves and their children with nutritious meals, well-heated and soundly constructed homes, and consistent medical and dental care. Communities characterized by poverty cannot provide sanitation systems, paved roads, public transportation, safe water sources, or networks of communication. An average American income, both on an individual and group basis, is needed before the American Indians, Aleuts, and Eskimos can be expected to reach the health status of the average American citizen.

CULTURAL PROBLEMS

Typical modern medical practices and traditional Indian culture are not generally compatible phenomena. Each tribal group is culturally distinct from another, and all are culturally different from that of "mainstream" America. Their language, social organization, religion, value structure, and mores often make it difficult for them to accept white medicine and for public health personnel to employ their usual methods of health care.

The Indian concept of health, while varying somewhat from tribe to tribe, often differs so vastly from a professional medical concept that the Indian must reject his cultural traditions in order to take advantage of the white man's medical prowess. Having relied upon and trusted medicine men for centuries, the Indian is understandably reluctant to accept a white physician as competent. Even the most "sophisticated" Indian is well aware of the white doctor's inability to cure emotional and mental disorders. Consequently there has evolved an interesting ideology of medicine among many Indian people. Those who have come to accept white medicine go to physicians for cures to overt physical ailments, such as broken bones, acute diseases with external symptoms, tuberculosis, and advanced stages of trachoma and malnutrition. Internal disorders and illnesses stemming from emotional problems are considered the jurisdiction of tribal medicine men. While there is little doubt that white medicine is more successful in curing most internal ailments, it is just as feasible that the medicine men are in a better position to solve problems of a mental or emotional nature among their own people.

Various manifestations of the Indian's orientation toward medicine are reported by medical health workers. A doctor for the Cherokees finds that his patients expect to receive some type of medicine every time they are examined and that it is difficult for him to persuade them to remove any article of clothing for physical examinations. A common problem seems to be that the Indian simply pays no attention to early warning signs of illness and merely accepts the discomfort as one of those things he must tolerate. When he finally does visit a physician, he cannot locate the source of his pain. It seems that many American Indians view sickness as an affliction of the entire body, and it requires lengthy questioning and examination for a doctor to discover the real medical problem.

Another physician on the Pine Ridge reservation reports that if medical instructions are interpreted as scolding, confrontation, or confusing, the Indians will always withdraw and fail to follow up an initial visit. It is an absolute rule on this reservation that anger, confusion, and arguments be avoided at all costs.[8] And public health workers on the Navajo reservation complain that few Indian mothers will return for postnatal care or regular medical checkups for their children.[9] Convalescence is another major problem for the physician. A doctor for the Northern Cheyennes finds it almost impossible to convince his patients to stay in bed to recuperate or not to ride a horse when they have a broken leg in a cast.[10]

BACKGROUND

The federal government's involvement in Indian health dates back to the early 1800s when the military forts established vaccination clinics for the native Americans in surrounding areas. The first direct federal appropriation for the health care of American Indians was made in the amount of $12,000 in 1832 to provide for physicians and vaccine supplies.[11] This reflects more self-interest than altruistic concern for the health of Indians. The War Department was primarily concerned with protecting soldiers from any communicable diseases carried by the Indians. Despite the near-universal inclusion of health and medical care in the treaties between the tribes and the United States government, the extent of attention to the health of the Indians depended entirely upon the availability of army doctors and surplus medical supplies.

In 1849 the federal health programs were transferred along with the rest of the Bureau of Indian Affairs from the War Department to the Department of the Interior. Perhaps the new nonmilitary atmosphere surrounding Indian health services prompted an increased interest in the programs, for a corps of health workers began to develop soon thereafter. By 1880 the Bureau of Indian Affairs ran four hospitals, provided the services of 80 physicians, and attempted to include preventive medicine in their activities. The following decade saw 25 nurses and service field matrons teaching hygiene and sanitation, providing emergency care, and prescribing medicine for minor illnesses in boarding schools and reservation communities.[12]

While the first chief medical supervisor was appointed in 1908, it was not until the early 1920s that a Health Division was established and district medical directors were employed. Programs for the control of specific diseases and supportive health education activities began at the turn of the century. In 1914 the first government medical care program for the Indians, Eskimos, and Aleuts was established in conjunction with the first territorial schools in Alaska. Five dentists were enlisted to visit schools and communities in 1913, and by 1928 sanitary engineers on loan to the BIA from the Public Health Service were researching reservation sanitation problems.

Efforts to transfer the federal health program from the Bureau of Indian Affairs to the Public Health Service began as early as 1919 when the proposal was made by the House Committee on Indian Affairs but opposed by both agencies. Repeated efforts to effect the transfer during the succeeding 36 years were opposed on the basis that health services for Indians might be deemphasized when taken from the agency whose sole concern was for Indian welfare. The Department of Health, Education, and Welfare voiced concern that the transfer might even accentuate Indian health problems, and the Bureau of the Budget argued that efficiency and effective administration would best be achieved if health services remained under the BIA.[13]

But the medical establishment favored the transfer to the Public Health Service, and its views prevailed in August 1954. Its spokesmen argued persuasively that the PHS had greater capability than the BIA to staff Indian health facilities and to obtain more adequate appropriations from Congress. Other arguments in favor of the transfer included the desire to eliminate existing duplication of federal health efforts and the belief that an agency in the Department of Health, Education, and Welfare would have a better chance of achieving state and local cooperation in the provision of health services for Indians.[14]

The savings anticipated from merging the Indian health program with other PHS efforts did not materialize. Over 2,500 personnel, 48 hospitals, and 13 school infirmaries were merely shifted in July 1955 from the BIA to the Public Health Service. Indian hospitals and health services were not merged with existing PHS facilities, and no hospitals were closed. Policies concerning eligibility for Indian health programs were unaltered by the transfer.

The Indian program of the Public Health Service continued to grow. A law passed in 1957 authorized funds for the construction of community hospitals and clinics to "serve Indians and non-Indians," and in 1959 the Surgeon General was authorized to provide and maintain personnel quarters for these hospitals and clinics and sanitation facilities for Indian homes and communities. By 1962 the division of the PHS, which is now called the Indian Health Service, had assumed all responsibility for federal Indian health services.

BUDGET AND ORGANIZATIONAL STRUCTURE

In its first year as the agency responsible for the health care of American Indians, the IHS spent $24.5 million, including $15.1 million for the operation of IHS hospitals and $3.2 million for field health programs. By fiscal 1971, congressional appropriations increased to $118 million, $63 million of which was for the operation of IHS hospitals and $30.6 million of which was for field health services. Contractual services quadrupled from 1955 to 1971 to increase the delivery of health services to Indians by public and private hospitals and doctors (Table 12). And in his July 8, 1970, message to Congress, President Nixon favored further expansion of Indian health services and requested the allocation of an additional $10 million annually for Indian health programs.[15]

The Indian Health Service attempts to accomplish its

Table 12. Obligations of Indian Health Service,
Selected Fiscal Years, 1950–1971
(MILLIONS)

	1955, ACTUAL	1960, ACTUAL	1965, ACTUAL	1970, ESTIMATE	1971, APPROPRIATED
Total	$24.5	$45.5	$62.7	$106.0	$118.0
Total patient care	20.1	36.1	49.3	76.9	85.2
Direct (operation Indian Health Service hospitals)	15.1	27.6	37.6	56.8	63.0
Indirect	5.0	8.6	11.7	20.1	22.2
Total field health	3.2	8.0	11.6	26.6	30.6
Sanitation	*	1.2	1.8	4.2	4.3
Dental	*	1.4	2.0	3.5	3.8
Public Health nursing	*	1.4	1.8	3.1	3.2
Health education	*	.4	.6	1.3	1.4
Field medical services	*	3.7	5.4	14.6	18.1
Menominee	—	—	—	.4	—
Administration	1.3	1.3	1.8	2.1	2.1

* Not available.
Note: Details do not necessarily add to totals because of rounding.
Source: Indian Health Service.

goals of delivering health services to Indians and Alaskan natives through a comprehensive program of health care. Its efforts include outpatient care, public health nursing, maternal and child care, dental and nutritional services, hospitalization, environmental services, health education, and the training of Indian health personnel.

The Indian Health Service, headquartered in Rockville, Maryland, is administratively divided into eight field areas. Within each field area are a number of service units, generally serving a particular reservation or several smaller ones. The Navajo Reservation, being the largest, is served by eight units. A service unit typically includes a hospital or health center and several medical and dental clinics.

Operating under the assumption that the individual unit is closer to the real needs of its service population, the Indian

Health Service stresses, at least in its rhetoric, the autonomy of the local unit in planning, implementing, and assessing its own programs whenever possible. While most federal agencies filter programs from the national level through intermediary ranks to the local level, spokesmen for the Indian Health Service claim that the agency reverses the process and builds the national plan from its component parts. This is an administratively new approach which has not yet been evaluated but which is viewed optimistically by IHS officials and tolerantly by HEW administrators.

The Indian Health Service restricts the delivery of medical services to approximately 425,000 Americans, mostly located on reservations in 23 states or in isolated Alaskan villages. IHS rarely attempts to follow its clients once they leave the reservations and move to the metropolitan areas. IHS maintains that it assures a "priority" to Indians living on or near a reservation, and thus far its funds have been too limited to extend its services beyond the priority target population. The illusive primary goal of the Indian Health Service is to bring these people up to "a level of health comparable to that of the general population."[16]

The number of Indians actually served by IHS is a matter of speculation. It is known that in fiscal 1968 there were about 92,000 admissions to Public Health Indian or contract hospitals, an average daily hospital population of nearly 3,000, and a total of 1.6 million outpatient visits to IHS hospitals and field clinics.[17] What is not known is the number of different individuals who were treated, for there currently is no tabulation accounting for multiple admissions or visits for a single case. It would seem reasonable that a person visiting a physician for any reason other than a routine check-up would require additional follow-up visits. It is also likely that a person who has enough confidence in the Public Health Service to seek its help once will return for subsequent visits. These two factors would cause an inflation in the number of visits and admissions without affecting the actual number of persons benefiting from the services of the Indian Health program.

PROGRAM COMPONENTS

Because the target population of the Indian Health Service encompasses many scattered villages and isolated families, it is necessary to have both direct and indirect programs. In mid-1970, the IHS operated 51 hospitals, ranging in size from 6 to 276, with a combined total capacity of 2,674 beds, and most with an outpatient department; 71 full-time health centers; and over 300 field health clinics. Two of the hospitals, one in Rapid City, South Dakota, and the other in Albuquerque, New Mexico, are tuberculosis sanatoriums. Three hospitals in Anchorage, Alaska, Gallup, New Mexico, and Phoenix, Arizona, are classified as medical centers, and they care for both patients from the surrounding areas and those referred for major surgery and special diagnostic, therapeutic, and rehabilitative treatment from other smaller Indian hospitals.

Besides operating reservation hospitals, the Indian Health Service administers an extensive field health program and several projects designed to attack specific health problems. The field health program is concerned with community and home services, environmental control, and preventive health care. Operating from hospitals, health centers, and clinics located as closely as possible to scattered and isolated Indians and Alaskan natives, field medical personnel provide such therapeutic care as diagnosis, treatment, referral, and follow-up care after hospitalization, and such preventive health services as prenatal and postnatal care, school health programs, screening and detection of disease, immunizations, and control of deficiency diseases and mental health.

The services of public health nurses, health educators,

medical social workers, nutritionists, sanitarians, and social work counselors are integrated into this program. All field health personnel, along with trained Indian community health representatives and aides, make regularly scheduled visits to private homes and field clinics in an effort to make health service more convenient and closer to the real needs of the Indian population.

The Indian Health Service nursing program includes the operation of a School of Practical Nursing for Indian girls as well as special courses to prepare practical nurses to assist public health nurses. The nurses, over 20 percent of whom are now Indians, are especially important in providing health service on reservations, for they work intimately with Indian families in their own homes.

To help counteract the negative influences of neglect, inadequate dental resources, and lack of understanding of dental care, the Indian Health Service provides professional dental services in hospitals, health centers, health stations, and 13 mobile dental units. In those locations where there are no Public Health facilities, private dentists are contracted or itinerant dental teams bring equipment with them on their regular visits. The primary thrust of the dental program is directed toward the younger population. In fiscal 1968 about 36 percent of the potential service population received dental care—over half of the under-20 population received treatment as compared with only one-sixth of those over 20 years of age receiving some type of care.

The environmental health program is potentially a most significant component of the entire Indian Health Service. Many serious respiratory and infectious diseases (either partially or entirely caused by overcrowded and substandard housing, scarce and often contaminated water supplies, and a lack of sewage and disposal facilities) could be prevented through large-scale improvements of the environmental conditions under which so many Indians live.

Until 1959, when the Indian Sanitation Facilities Act (Pub. L. No. 86-121) was passed, environmental health activities were largely confined to infrequent inspections of reservation sanitation facilities and a school educational program. The new law authorized the Surgeon General to enter into contracts and agreements with Indians to construct and maintain water supply, drainage, waste disposal, and other facilities for homes, communities, and reservations. Sanitation facilities were provided for more than half of the families by 1970. During the first nine years under this legislation, 613 construction projects (170 of which serve federal housing projects) and 151 engineering investigations, emergency work, and other special projects serving about 44,000 families were completed. Work has since accelerated so that a total of 914 construction projects alone were completed from the beginning of the program through the end of fiscal 1970. Since 1960, some 60,000 families have been provided running water and waste-disposal systems.

The Indian Health Service also operates several programs designed to attack particular health problems. A five-year trachoma-control program emphasizes the prevention of further spread among the Indian population of this serious eye disease. A maternal and child care program emphasizes early prenatal care for the mother and continuing care for both mother and child after birth. While the infant death rate among Indian and Alaskan natives declined 48 percent between 1955 and 1967, their rate is still 1.44 times higher than that of the general U.S. population. Maternal death rates per 100,000 live births among Indians and Alaskan natives has declined from 90 in 1962 to 34 in 1967, but remains 1.2 times higher than that of the total U.S. population.[18]

By the end of fiscal 1970, there were 76,700 reservation Indian women between the ages of 15 and 44, and nearly half of them received some form of birth-control devices. The majority chose the "pill" and half as many selected the intrauterine device (IUD); but preferences varied among the tribes. For example, Navajo women chose the IUD over all other devices by a ratio of 2 to 1. Navajos appear to reject the consumption of any kind of pill and the tribal medicine men counsel against the use of oral contraceptives.

Former Secretary of the Interior Udall pioneered the birth-control program in 1965 when he became the first Cabinet officer to announce a family planning policy, and the number of users increased more than ninefold in the next five years to 36,000. The effectiveness of the program is reflected in the consequent decrease in the number of recorded Indian births in Public Health hospitals, which declined from 9,500 in 1965 to 8,900 in 1969.

While the IHS does profess to have a special mental health program, it is hardly adequate to treat the many emotional disorders caused by severe cultural conflict between traditional Indian society and the dominant white society. Nearly 3,000 Indians are hospitalized for psychiatric disorders each year; the suicide rate is about 15 percent higher than the rest of the U.S. population; the homicide rate is three times greater. As "accidents" cause over 20 percent of the deaths among Indians and only 6 percent among the total United States population,[19] there is reason to suspect that the incidence of mental illness (especially mental illness contributing to suicidal tendencies) is even higher than estimated. Efforts are increasing in the field of mental health. While only four reservations were served by mental health teams in 1967, all IHS areas were provided with the teams by 1970.

PERSONNEL

The Indian Health Service employed about 5,500 persons in 1970 plus about 1,000 commissioned corps doctors and dentists, but many are assigned to various administrative positions and are not directly involved in the provision of health services. Three of every four IHS employees are Indians, mostly concentrated in the lower civil service position.

There were 108 physicians for every 100,000 reservation Indians in 1970, as compared with 164 for the total population, and one dentist for every 3,400 Indians, as compared with one for every 1,900 for the United States. While the ratios of medical professionals to Indians do not differ too drastically from that of the population as a whole and are significantly better than those in most isolated areas, it is not sufficient to bring the health of Indian people up to U.S. standards. More specialized personnel are needed to help alleviate the serious gap between Indian and white health conditions.

Though productivity measurements are not available, it is questionable whether the performance of IHS physicians can be compared with doctors who are settled in the communities they serve. Medical professionals are reluctant to leave modern hospital facilities to practice in isolated and poorly equipped reservation medical centers. Consequently, most IHS doctors are young men who are satisfying their two-year military obligation by working with the Public Health Service. Shortages of nurses are common even in urban, established hospitals, and their inadequate supply on reservations is chronic. Inadequate technical and medical facilities and supplies, poor housing facilities, lack of cultural and recreational amenities, and language barriers are responsible for the acute shortages of health workers on reservations; and they are not likely to be overcome in the foreseeable future.

In an effort to overcome the difficulties of delivering health services to its clientele, the IHS contracts for the services of private and state hospitals and private practitioners. Contract services provide specialized diagnostic and therapeutic care not available in PHS hospitals and offer persons living in isolated areas medical care. In addition to contracting with about 500 privately practicing doctors and dentists and for about 1,000 hospital beds in 300 community hospitals and state and local tuberculosis and mental hospitals, the IHS has contractual arrangements with 18 state and local health departments for various public health services, including nursing, sanitation, tuberculosis, and communicable disease control. Also utilized on a reimbursement basis are such other federal facilities as Veterans Administration, military, and non-Indian Public Health Service facilities.

The decision to contract services is based upon the quality of available resources. If the IHS feels that a contractual arrangement can best meet the needs of a particular area or program, it will pay an outside doctor and/or hospital for services. About $20 million, or almost a fifth of the total IHS budget in 1970, was spent for contract care.

While the number of Indians making use of these contracts has been increasing, there remains a widespread mistrust of non-Indian hospitals among reservation people. Aside from language problems, Indians claim that they frequently receive inferior treatment in contracted facilities. A wide selection of contract hospitals, however, is not always available to IHS since many private and state hospitals are reluctant or unwilling to enter into a contract in which they will be required to treat Indians. With the inception of Medicare and Medicaid, however, some of these hospitals have been forced to eliminate discriminatory practices to ensure government funding.

The Indian Health Service also cooperates with other federal agencies, universities, and independent organizations in the planning, funding, and implementation of health projects. There is, however, little coordination between IHS and the other agencies that operate related programs.

Naturally enough, some IHS efforts most closely parallel those of the Bureau of Indian Affairs. For example, the two agencies work together to plan and implement school health programs conducted in boarding and day schools operated by the BIA.

PARTICIPATION

The charge of paternalism has been leveled against IHS as well as against the BIA, although the IHS insists that its orientation is to work *with* and *for* the Indian population. And militant demands have accelerated IHS attempts to "involve" Indians in the running of their own health facilities.

An essential ingredient in securing Indian participation in the administration and operation of their own health facilities is the training of Indians to fill positions of responsibility in delivering health care. The training also serves the additional role of qualifying Indians to fill health jobs for which there is an inadequate supply of candidates. The Indian Health Service allocated $1.2 million in fiscal 1970 to train more than 500 Indians to fill various health jobs, including technicians, practical nurses, sanitation aides, and related occupations. For example, an Alaskan community-oriented training project offered a 10-week course to 185 village-selected trainees to qualify them to serve as auxiliary IHS health workers in areas where health resources would not otherwise be available. Even if the training programs are successful, at best they will prepare Indians to serve in subordinate positions in the health industry. The IHS is aware that to offer Indians the opportunity to gain eventual control over their health care facilities, professional medical training must be provided. Thus far, the IHS has allocated few resources to this crucial preparation for self-determination in the area of health care, and there is little evidence that special efforts have been made to offer financial inducement for Indian students to pursue professional medical careers.

The IHS has, however, encouraged Indians to serve in an advisory capacity on boards which help administer health facilities. The basic function of the various boards is to work with the federal staff in planning, operating, and evaluating the various program efforts of the IHS. The activities of the advisory boards are coordinated by the National Indian Health Service Advisory Committee. Once consisting entirely of white medical doctors and other professionals, the Committee by 1970 contained six Indians (one of whom is a physician) and three white health professionals. The two latest additions to the Committee were selected by the Indians themselves. Participation on advisory boards, however, is not to be equated with control over operations. The purse strings and control are still held by federal officials. The health advisory boards have only as much decision-making powers as the IHS officials allow them to exercise, and few Indians have qualified to fill professional positions in health services.

AN ASSESSMENT

Despite the progress achieved during recent years, the health status of American Indians is far from satisfactory. They are more often victims of disease than other poverty stricken groups in the United States, and great numbers even suffer from illnesses rarely found among other peoples. Reservation residents have a higher infant mortality rate, a shorter life expectancy, and a greater incidence of hunger and malnutrition than other rural poor in the nation.

While the general health of Indians is poor, it has been worse. And credit for most of the improvements must go to the Indian Health Service which has consistently, though slowly, contributed to better health conditions on this country's reservations and to Congress which has more than quadrupled appropriations for Indian health care since 1955. Since the IHS assumed responsibility for America's Indians, Aleuts, and Eskimos in 1955, admissions to PHS Indian and contract hospitals increased 84 percent by 1968. Outpatient visits to hospitals, clinics, and health centers have more than tripled, and the number of dental services provided has nearly quadrupled. Once the greatest killer of Indian and Alaskan natives, the incidence rates of tuberculosis have been drastically reduced since 1955. While the incidence of tuberculosis among Indians and Alaskan natives remains over four times the U.S. rate, new active Indian tuberculosis cases declined by 33.6 percent between 1955 and 1968.

The infant mortality rate among Indians and Alaskan natives declined about 48 percent between 1955 and 1967, from 62.5 to 32.2 per thousand live births. During this same period, the rate for the total United States population dropped by 15 percent. Still the infant death rate remains 1.4 times as large as the average American rate, and for Alaskan natives the death rate is even higher than for Indians. The gap between the life expectancies of Indians and the total population is also narrowing. While the Indian life expectancy was 60.0 years as compared with 68.2 for the rest of the population in 1950, it was 64.0 as compared with 70.5 for the total population by 1967.

Not to be overlooked are the many contributing factors which serve to accentuate the health problems of American Indians. The average reservation family lives in a one- or two-room house, often lacking running water and adequate means of waste disposal. The higher Indian infant mortality rate is probably partly due to deaths in the postnatal period when infants leave the hospital and are brought to their impoverished home environments. A large number of illnesses requiring medical attention are due to infectious diseases and their residuals that fester and grow in overcrowded and unsanitary conditions. Dental problems among

Indian children are caused by improper diets and parental inattention to dental care. The average Indian child between the ages of 6 and 17 experiences 6 more decayed teeth than white and black children. Isolation and the lack of adequate transportation inhibits the ability of many Indians to attend health clinics or hospitals for regular checkups, and low literacy and educational levels make understanding good health practices more difficult.

Many of these problems are outside the scope of the IHS. Some of the problems of delivering adequate health care to American Indians are problems common to health care in the entire nation. There is a shortage of health manpower throughout the country as well as a general lack of knowledge as to the most effective method of delivery of comprehensive health services to rural, isolated, or disadvantaged populations. Additional funds would help alleviate the situation, though that alone would not solve most of the acute problems. Many IHS hospitals fail to meet fire and safety codes and the demands for hospital space and beds, not to mention minimal requirements of accreditation standards by professional societies. Current construction plans are barely adequate to maintain and repair existing buildings and do not provide for the erection or replacement of new facilities. Additional funds would be necessary to expand facilities. Bringing up Indian health standards to the level of the white American population is a staggering and complex challenge. More money and facilities would help but would not be sufficient to achieve this goal.

Housing, employment, education, sanitation, industry, and nutrition are all inextricably related to advancement in health. It will require the sustained and concerted efforts of the Indians and their tribal comrades and agencies in the federal, state, and local governments to bring the health standards of Indians to the level of the rest of the population.

NOTES

1. U.S. Department of Health, Education, and Welfare, Public Health Service, *A Review of the Indian Health Program,* February 9, 1967, p. 4. (Mimeographed.)

2. "Summary of the Fourth National Conference on Indian Health Sponsored by the Association on American Indian Affairs," U.S. Congress, Senate, Committee on Labor and Public Welfare, *Indian Education,* Part 1, before a Special Subcommittee on Indian Education, 90th Cong., 1st and 2nd Sess., 1967–68, p. 59.

3. Statement of Dr. Jean Van Dusen before U.S. Congress, Senate, Committee on Labor and Public Welfare, ibid., p. 216.

4. "Indians' Problems Challenge Physicians," *The AMA News,* June 9, 1969.

5. "For Healthier Little Indians," *Today's Health,* July 1965.

6. U.S. Department of Health, Education, and Welfare, Public Health Service, *Indian Health Trends and Services,* 1969, pp. 12 and 30.

7. Footnote 1.

8. Luis Kemnitzer, "Whiteman Medicine, Indian Medicine, and Indian Identity on Pine Ridge Reservation, South Dakota," U.S. Congress, Senate, Committee on Labor and Public Welfare, *Indian Education,* Part IV, before a Special Subcommittee on Indian Education, 90th Cong., 1st and 2nd Sess., 1968, p. 1309.

9. Footnote 5.

10. Glenn Sumpter, "White Medicine Man," *The New Physician,* May 1966.

11. Act of May 5, 1832, 4 Stat. 514.

12. U.S. Department of Health, Education, and Welfare, Public Health Service, *The Indian Health Program of the U.S. Public Health Service,* 1969, pp. 17–18.

13. U.S. Congress, Senate, Committee on Interior and Insular Affairs, *Transfer of Indian Hospitals and Health Facilities to Public Health Service,* Hearings on H.R. 303, 83rd Cong., 2d Sess., 1954, p. 9.

14. U.S. Department of Health, Education, and Welfare, Public Health Service, *The Indian Health Program from 1800–1955,* Mar. 11, 1959, pp. 25–26.

15. U.S. Congress, House, "The American Indians—Message from the President of the United States," *Congressional Record,* daily ed., 91st Cong., 2d Sess., July 8, 1970, p. H6440.

16. Cited in William A. Brophy and Sophie D. Aberle, *The Indian: America's Unfinished Business,* University of Oklahoma Press, Norman, Oklahoma, 1966, p. 161.

17. Footnote 1, pp. 48–52.

18. Ibid., pp. 8–9.

19. Ibid., p. 16.

"THE GREAT KING TOLD ME THE PATH SHOULD NEVER BE CROOKED, BUT OPEN FOR EVERY ONE TO PASS AND REPASS. AS WE ALL LIVE IN ONE LAND, I HOPE WE SHALL ALL LOVE ONE PEOPLE."—LITTLE CARPENTER

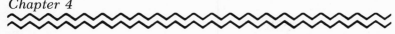

Chapter 4

Developing Community Structure

COMMUNITY ORGANIZATION

Consistent with the historical Big Brother policy of the Bureau of Indian Affairs, the caretaker institution of the nation's Indian population has made little effort to help in the development of Indian community organizations. Under the traditional philosophy of providing *for* the Indians, there has been no need for a process by which a group of people improve the quality of their living condition through collective control over their own affairs. The status of community organization in the BIA scheme of things is reflected in the fact that the agency did not see fit to appoint a community development officer until 1968, and he still does not have the funds or the status in the agency that would allow him to help develop local initiative within tribal communities.

OEO INITIATIVE

While the Bureau of Indian Affairs and other federal agencies have always earmarked all funds spent on reservations

Top: *Adult education at a Twin Lakes, New Mexico, Navajo reservation. The Crawford family learning word association memory course.* Bottom: *Navajo Tribal Chapter meeting at Indian Wells.*

for programs designed in Washington, the Office of Economic Opportunity (OEO) was the first to make grants to reservation groups for programs largely of their own design. OEO deserves much of the credit for demonstrating the value, indeed the necessity, of allowing Indians to create and implement community activities with minimal interference from federal agencies. This agency gave self-determination and Indian community organization the initial impetus. The BIA and other federal agencies soon began to stress these same objectives, though they have been extremely slow in relinquishing authority over the programs they administer.

The Indian Community Action Program (ICAP) shares the formal goal of all OEO antipoverty programs—the stimulation of local initiative through the organization of community action agencies, the development of remedial programs, the improvement of delivery services to the poor, the utilization of existing resources through the coordination of public and private services, and the improvement of employment capability and general economic well-being. The initial objective of the ICAP was the encouragement of indigenous participation and the concomitant stimulation of local leadership development. As most federally chartered tribal governments are comparable to municipal and county governments, they provided a ready-made apparatus for the rapid creation of community action agencies. And the long history of dependence upon government programs found on the reservation further facilitated the early establishment of OEO programs. Within a few months following the passage of the Economic Opportunity Act in 1964, many tribal councils had adopted resolutions to authorize community action agencies and had designated themselves as Community Action Agency (CAA) boards.

An Indian Branch within OEO's Office of Special Field Programs was established to facilitate program development. Though OEO was not adequately staffed or funded to achieve its goal of establishing a CAA on every reservation, the agency took the position that it could not refuse assistance to the poor and funded most of the ICAPs on a "first come, first served" basis. Within three years after the agency was established, it supported 67 community action agencies on 170 reservations with a population in excess of 300,000.

Both programs and their funding vary from reservation to reservation. Indian community action agencies have generally been allowed more local initiative in the formulation of their programs than have other community action agencies. While many of the local components are unique to particular reservations, there are some programs that have been especially popular. Whether the repetition of "packaged" projects is a result of expediency and administrative convenience or independent proposals of several reservations remains a source of controversy. There is, however, little question that most Indian reservations are badly in need of the same housing, community organization, economic development, and manpower assistance. The mere presence of similar program components on several reservations may indicate that they serve the purposes and the needs of most Indian communities. It is doubtful that community agencies would request funds for a component that is not needed when the money could be applied to so many other constructive projects.

Project Head Start, designed to prepare four- and five-year-olds for entry into school, was the largest component of ICAP until fiscal 1970 when the program was transferred to the U.S. Office of Education. In 1970, there were 59 reservations with Head Start projects and about 10,000 preschool participants. Another nationally popular program, Legal Services, enlists attorneys to represent poor Indians and Indian groups when they cannot afford other legal counsel; attempts to reform the law where it is vague, destructively complex, or contrary to the interest of the community; and encourages Indian participation in the formulation, interpretation, and utilization of legal doctrine. In 1970, there were Legal Service projects on seven reservations plus a regional project serving all California Indians.

OEO has supported diverse activities under its community organization program, ranging from ICAP administration and planning to support of neighborhood services and technical assistance to communities. Total support of community organization activities has been rising, and the $7 million expended on the program in fiscal 1970 made it the largest single component of OEO aid to reservations (Table 13).

Health programs, often closely coordinated with the Indian Health Service of the Department of Health, Education, and Welfare, included projects devoted to environmental health, alcoholism prevention and control, and medical services. OEO's education program supported basic education for adults, remedial and supplementary work for children, and "community education" in the form of consumer education, citizen participation, and community develop-

Table 13. Indian Community Action Program Expenditures, 1967–1970

PROGRAM	AMOUNT (MILLIONS)			
	1967	1968	1969	1970
Total	$20.1	$22.3	$24.4	$22.2
Community organization	3.7	3.6	5.9	7.0
Education	2.2	2.5	.6	3.9
Health	1.4	1.4	1.5	3.5
Manpower	—	—	1.7	1.8
Special programs	.7	2.4	1.7	1.7
Housing	3.6	4.3	4.4	1.5
Legal Services	.3	.7	1.2	1.5
Economic development	.5	.7	1.1	1.4
Head Start	7.7	6.7	6.4	.1

Source: Office of Economic Opportunity.

ment lessons. Economic development and manpower programs, like their larger counterparts administered by BIA, Labor, and the Economic Development Administration, focused on the encouragement of employers to locate on or near reservations.

Not all OEO assistance to reservations was administered through Indian community action agencies. Volunteers in Service to America (VISTA) assigned 194 volunteers to 28 reservation projects in 1970 at an annual field cost of $3,804 per volunteer. Most of the volunteers worked through the reservation CAAs where they launched literacy programs, started libraries and recreational programs for youth, and organized preschool and self-help housing projects. VISTA workers have in many cases been responsible for bringing injustices, hardships, and special problems to the attention of private or governmental agencies that have the power, resources, and responsibility to take corrective action.

Another program funded directly by OEO at an annual cost of about $1.4 million is the Consortium, including four Western universities and three tribal groups, whose staff provided technical assistance in planning and drafting proposals, organizing the ICAPs and implementing their programs, training agency staff, and providing other services. OEO's Research and Demonstration Division funded a special scholarship program in law for American Indians at the University of New Mexico, a school administration program to offer master of arts degrees in school administration to Indian teachers at four universities, and the development of Indian urban service centers.

While ICAP officials have not yet supplied quantitative support for their claims, it is speculated that experience received by the Indians as they serve on ICAP staffs, governing boards, and program teams has led to increased interest and participation in community affairs. More apparent is the contribution OEO has made to accelerating fundamental changes in BIA funding practices.

OEO spokesmen claim that the programs have had an influence on keeping the younger tribal members on the reservation by their promises of jobs, recreation, and a future in the leadership of their own people in a significant manner through obtaining tribal offices, program administrative positions, and jobs with private corporations locating on reservations. And certainly the short-run effects of employment, diet supplementation, early childhood education, new homes, and community organizations are immeasurable, but obviously beneficial, to the Indian people.

The Indian Community Action Program is not without its difficulties. Because the sponsoring agency on the reservation is normally the tribal government, it has been suggested that old "establishment" ideas are being supported rather than new and innovative plans for the future. OEO reservation officials have been criticized for incorporating more prepackaged plans than projects tailored to the unique needs of individual reservations. And many projects, both newly created and older but still popular, have not been funded as requested by OEO.

The long-range effect of the Indian OEO programs is not yet known, but it is doubtful whether they can lift an appreciable number of Indians out of poverty under existing conditions and levels of federal expenditure. Given the very serious and extensive needs of the Indian community, many more homes will have to be built, children educated, jobs created, and industries established before the centuries-old conditions of poverty on this country's reservations can be eliminated. And this would require a comprehensive national approach, supported by adequate funds and involving Indian leadership and participation, and not just a series of OEO programs, regardless of how successful they might individually be.

While the past record of BIA support of community organization has been disappointing, there is reason to believe that the situation will improve in the near future. Commissioner of Indian Affairs Louis Bruce favors moves toward increasing independence and self-control for reservation communities, and an Indian director of community development was appointed in 1971.

The ultimate goal of self determination among reservation communities requires basic and radical structural changes within the federal-Indian relationship. True community organization is only possible when portions of the power now held by Bureau officials can be transferred into local positions. No new legislation is necessary to implement self-determination. Under the "Buy Indian" provisions of 1910, the BIA is authorized to negotiate with tribal authorities for community organization service contracts and to allow Indian tribes to assume management over an increasing range of programs, services, and municipal functions that have previously been provided by the Bureau of Indian Affairs and other federal agencies.

Some actual accomplishments in this direction have been effected during recent years, even though most of the community development activity has been in the area of planning and policy formulation. The Ramah agreement, through which the BIA is providing the Ramah Navajo School Board the operating funds, paved the way for other reservations to negotiate with the BIA and take the option to control their own schools. The eight Pueblos were authorized to hire outside consultants with BIA funds, and the Zuñi tribe took advantage of an old law permitting the tribal organization to supervise BIA officials on their reservation. However, so long as the BIA is granted control over federal funds by Congress and Bureau officials remain responsible for the expenditure of federal appropriations, it is doubtful whether the much-publicized authority granted to the Zuñis will result in the transfer of power to tribal representatives.

Proponents of the new push toward Indian self-determination within the BIA stress that community organization must be accompanied not only by an attitude that encourages and supports tribal responsibility for decision-making and program-making and program-planning and implementation, but also by congressional recognition that Indians should control their own communities. Obviously, BIA officialdom cannot be eliminated suddenly since they perform vital functions, but a concerted effort must be made to allow the tribes to assume full responsibility with a minimum of assistance from the federal government.

The response of some BIA officials concerned with community organization on the reservation has been to bolster the bureaucracy by the appointment of experienced community development officers to help the tribes develop their own communities. But another bureaucratic layer is hardly a key to self-determination. A National Community Development Committee composed of community development representatives from the BIA Washington office, area directors, assistant area directors, agency superintendents, and area community development officers is already in existence but is totally inactive. In theory, the function of the committee is to advise the Commissioner on community development affairs, direct training activities, and establish the guidelines under which community development contracts and grants will be made. But so long as BIA hierarchy clings to its powers to control tribal life, there is little that another BIA committee can do.

Perhaps the most potentially significant component of the proposed community development scheme is the granting of contracts and money awards to Indian tribes. The major criterion controlling the awarding of grants and contracts will be the degree to which the proposed activity will lead to tribal control over previously federally administered programs and funds. A few token contracts have already been granted, but the BIA has retained responsibility for administration of the projects. The school board of the Blackwater Day School received one of the contracts while the Salt River Pima tribes received three—for social services, management, and law and order—and the eight-member All Indian Pueblo Council has contracted for an educational counselor to process higher education grants.

While the BIA has been exasperatingly slow in implementing projects that might lead to greater self-determination, the obstacles should not be minimized. Tribal groups are not necessarily clamoring for self-control, and sensitivity to termination moves causes reservation officials to be reluctant to take unspecified funds. Experience has taught them to be suspicious of direct government funding, lest this type of funding would lead to federal relinquishment of responsibility. Surely any significant and widespread changes will depend upon altered attitudes and policies among both bureaucrats and Indians.

LAW AND ORDER

A legal system and the order it makes possible are essential ingredients of any community organization. The law and order aspect of a community's structure provides it with a code of human conduct that its members recognize as binding and reflects the community's expectations of acceptable behavior. Therefore, the legal system helps the community establish social order and effective control over the behavior of its members, thus maintaining predictability and cohesion within the organization.

LAW

There are three legal codes in operation on reservations—federal, state, and tribal. While the jurisdiction of each of the three codes is fairly well defined, they are not mutually exclusive, and all three can be applied in a single case. Some laws make no distinctions between Indians and other groups or individuals whether they are on or off the reservation; others are interpreted according to whether the offender or victim is Indian and where the offense is committed.

Certain federal criminal and civil laws that apply to all citizens of the United States are equally applicable to Indians whether they are on or off the reservation. The only acts of Indians against Indians in Indian country that are considered federal cases are the ten major crimes of rape, assault with the intention to kill, arson, murder, manslaughter, burglary, larceny against person or property,[1] incest, robbery, and assault with a deadly weapon,[2] plus embezzlement of tribal funds and the infringement of some federal statutes. Federal law is exercised in instances in which an Indian commits against a non-Indian on reservation property one of the ten major crimes or other serious offenses that would violate state law if committed off the reservation. Also belonging to the federal judiciary are all offenses committed by non-Indians against Indians on reservations.

State laws are in effect whenever an Indian commits a crime or is the victim of a crime off the reservation. This includes traffic violations; sales, excise and general property taxes; contracts; and the recovery of damages from injuries. State legislation is generally not applicable on the reservation unless Congress has explicitly conferred such jurisdiction or unless the tribe has been formally terminated.

There are other relationships that reservation Indians have with the state. Rent is paid on state grazing land; welfare payments and other social services are granted to Indians;

and automobile and drivers' licenses are obtained from state agencies. Both state and tribal licenses are required of non-Indians who desire to hunt or fish on tribal property. State laws are also applicable in situations involving a non-Indian against another non-Indian or his property on reservation land.

The laws of the tribe are supreme in cases involving offenses between Indians in Indian country unless the particular crime is included among the federal offenses. Exclusive jurisdiction is claimed by tribal authorities in such areas as simple assault and battery, disorderly conduct, adultery, prostitution, failure to support dependents, intoxication, thefts, fraud, trespassing, and blackmailing. Those offenses that do not involve a victim are subject only to federal or tribal laws.

While the law prohibits discrimination against Indians by officials and public organizations, law enforcement officials are often more strict in their administration of the law when Indians are the offenders than when they are the victims or when two non-Indians are involved. Indians must often enforce their right to vote and are rarely called for jury duty. Non-Indians committing crimes against Indians or on Indian property are often not convicted because the federal courts pay little attention to petty offenders. Furthermore, some areas of law are confusing because they have largely been unexplored or unclarified by past action, and local officials capitalize on the confusion to the detriment of Indians. Such is the case with the offenses involving no victim committed by non-Indians on reservations. The entire relationship between states and reservations, moreover, is also unclear.

Many law authorities believe that Indian codes of law are directed more toward rehabilitation than are state and federal laws. Most Indian codes define only fifty or so transgressions (compared with over 2,000 for most states). Sentences rarely exceed six months, and the performance of some task for the benefit of the tribe is a sentence preferred to imprisonment.[3]

As the legal code for Indian Americans is divided into three jurisdictions, so is the court system by which the transgression of the law is adjudicated. When the appropriate jurisdiction is not obvious, the court adjudicating an Indian case decides whether it is the jurisdiction of federal, state, or tribal authority, with federal legislation prevailing and tribal customs receiving secondary preference. Only when both of these systems fail to prescribe a law is state law considered applicable.[4]

To avoid local prejudices and judges under local political pressure, Indians choose federal district courts whenever they can make a case for federal jurisdiction or appeal a negative ruling to federal courts. A federal case must involve a defendant and a plaintiff from two different states and an amount exceeding $10,000 or come under the Constitution or federal laws and treaties before it can be tried in a federal court of law.

Because tribes are not considered citizens, they cannot satisfy the requirement of diversity of citizenship necessary to bring a case under federal jurisdiction. However, Indian groups were given the power under the Reorganization Act to protect their property through federal court appeals.

Whenever the United States government is the plaintiff, suits are handled in federal district courts. Indian tribal interests can also be protected in federal courts when the federal government intervenes in a case between two states before the Supreme Court.

Whether or not a case may be tried in state courts varies among the states with Indian reservation populations. The general policy established by Justice Marshall in 1832 that Indian tribes are dependent nations in whose territory state law does not apply is still followed, though some modifications have been allowed by Congress when the basic rights of Indians are not in jeopardy and when tribal relations are not involved.

Tribal courts generally have the authority to try civil cases. They have the power to adjudicate such cases as family law, torts, property, wills, heirship, suits between members of the tribe, and suits brought by persons not members of the tribe against tribal members or the tribe itself. Tribes have exclusive jurisdiction in these areas unless Congress explicitly gives it to the state.

The tribunals of tribes under the Reorganization Act enforce relevant federal statutes, Department of the Interior dictates, and those customs and ordinances not prohibited by the federal government. Because tribal decisions are not recorded in local or state offices, they are only enforceable outside of the reservation when brought to a state court. This process is seldom enacted since it is costly, time consuming, and undermines the authority of the tribal courts.

The person or persons charged with the responsibility of trying cases on reservations varies from reservation to reservation. In some instances, tribes will hire outside lawyers to judge a particular transgression. Larger and wealthier tribes, such as the Navajos and Utes, conduct special programs to train tribal judges and court personnel, but rarely are they professional attorneys who have completed law school and passed the state bar examinations. Indeed, some tribes have specific laws which prohibit a professional lawyer from participating in the tribunal.

Similarly, tribal justice systems vary widely according to the unique problems, customs, and resources of the tribes. The Navajo tribe, for instance, spends over a million dollars annually for law and order, including salaries for seven tribal judges, a jail system, and a large police force. Smaller tribes have no funds to spend for law and court systems, have no incarceration facilities, and weak enforcement procedures. Criticisms most often voiced concerning Indian judicial systems are: poorly educated and trained judges, inadequate equipment, lack of facilities for female and juvenile offenders, insufficient rights of appeal, favoritism, outdated detention facilities, and widespread practice of prohibiting lawyers to represent those individuals on trial.

Suggestions that responsibility for law enforcement on reservations be turned over to state jurisdictions frequently ignore the fact that lack of resources is likely to inhibit any chance of improvement on the tribal system in some states. Except for a few larger reservations, it remains equally doubtful that tribes can develop viable judicial systems to protect the rights of individuals and serve the needs of their communities.

THE BIA LAW AND ORDER PROGRAM

Wherever states do not have jurisdiction, the Bureau of Indian Affairs is responsible for the maintenance of law and order on Indian reservations. In fiscal 1970, the BIA spent about $5 million to provide for crime and delinquency prevention, investigations and enforcement, courts, jails, and rehabilitation to serve a population of 280,000 Indians on 83 reservations in 14 states.

Crime is a serious social problem on reservations. BIA statistics show that reported crimes have increased over 20 percent from 1966 to 1970 and are expected to reach 94,000 per year during fiscal 1971. Corresponding increases also occurred in arrests, detentions, court cases, and related law and order activities. To obtain a clearer perspective of the extent of crime on the reservation, a comparison with the crime rate in a metropolitan area might be helpful. The reported crimes (excluding all traffic violations except driving while intoxicated) on the reservations served by the BIA law and order program numbered 68,981 in 1969 compared with 94,635 crimes reported in the District of Columbia, for example, during the same year. Thus, an Indian population one-third that of the District reported nearly three-fourths the total number of crimes. And because of a lack of telephone communications, an absence of paved roads, scattered populations, and limited staff, Indian police are not able to be of as much assistance on reservations as metropolitan police in urbanized areas.

The BIA, partially because of a lack of funds, places little emphasis on the rehabilitation of offenders and devotes most of its efforts toward law enforcement. Despite the fact that Bureau law and order officials report that recidivism is common, funds and staff time are not allocated for crime prevention activities. BIA personnel recognize that the current circular procedure of jailing offenders, releasing them, and re-arresting the same persons is self-defeating. The recidivism rate of those Indian releasees from federal prisons who have entered BIA institutional training or have been directly employed under the BIA program is about 10 percent as compared with a national average of 50 percent. Only 178 persons, 116 of whom are still in the program, have been assisted by the Bureau through a 1967 agreement with the Bureau of Prisons, and only those in federal institutions and San Quentin in California are eligible. Even if the releasees who participate in the program are chosen especially for their potential for success in the outside world, the statistics suggest the program is worth expanding. In the Englewood Prison near Denver, for example, the recidivism dropped from over 80 percent to 9.5 percent with the initiation of the BIA assistance program. These data suggest the effectiveness of rehabilitation efforts and the need to expand investments in programs that focus on crime prevention and rehabilitation.

Tribal contributions nearly matched the $4.9 million the BIA spent for its law and order program in fiscal 1970, bringing the total per capita expenditure for law and order on the reservation to about $33. Aside from routine police activities, the BIA supported the Indian Police Academy at Roswell, New Mexico. This school graduated 138 officers in 4 different training sessions of 10 weeks' duration each. The Bureau has also held several workshops for Indian court judges to help upgrade the quality of judicial services and familiarize judges with the 1968 Indian Civil Rights Act.

WELFARE ASSISTANCE AND SERVICES

Welfare assistance is an important community function on the reservation because poverty, ill health, unemployment, and low levels of educational attainment are pervasive in these areas. The federal government supports four categorical assistance programs: Old Age Assistance, Aid to the Blind, Aid to the Permanently and Totally Disabled, and Aid to Families with Dependent Children. Most states offer some residual assistance to the poor who fail to qualify under any of these four categories, and localities share in the costs of the general assistance programs. The categorical public assistance programs are largely administered by the states, and subject to broad federal guidelines, the states determine eligibility standards and the level of benefits.

The Bureau of Indian Affairs is often forced to assume the responsibility for providing general assistance to those Indians not qualifying for categorical aid. This is because needy Indians often do not qualify under state eligibility requirements; because state established need standards are often far below actual minimal living costs; and because many states simply fail to provide for Indians as adequately as they do for the rest of their populations.

The Bureau of Indian Affairs welfare efforts are presumably residual, and they are supposed to supply a safety net when other forms of assistance fail or are unavailable. Indians (whether they live on reservations or elsewhere) are entitled to the same welfare benefits as other citizens of their respective states. However, serious gaps exist in many states, and Indians are frequently denied even the forms of assistance that are available to the general population because of their isolation or because of discriminatory practices. Many local areas in which Indians constitute a large portion of the population are unable to fund the necessary level of assistance because the tax-exempt Indian lands do not contribute to local revenues and because of the Indians' low incomes. Therefore, the BIA's Division of Social Services tries to provide essential services and assistance for reservation Indians whenever they are unavailable from state or local agencies.

The states of Washington, Oregon, Kansas, and California, where most of the Indians live on tiny rancherias or enclaves, assume the responsibility for the welfare of their Indian populations. The responsibility for social services on larger, isolated reservations is largely a function of the BIA. The Bureau also provides itinerant services to Eskimos and Aleuts who live in small, often nomadic, communities.

PUBLIC ASSISTANCE

Public assistance looms large in Indian life. Nearly 10 percent of the total Indian cash income comes from various forms of public assistance, paid either by the states or the BIA. As is true for the rest of the nation, public assistance is playing an increasingly important role in the lives of poor people and an even larger part for Indians because they are subject to more than their share of poverty. Since states do not maintain separate records on Indians receiving public assistance, the exact numbers being aided are unknown. Assuming a total of 90,000 families under BIA jurisdiction, about 3 of every 10 Indian families received federally supported categorical public assistance in 1969. Despite the growth of private and public employment on Indian reservations, the number of Aid to Families with Dependent Children (AFDC) recipients rose from 39,000 in 1966 to 46,000 in 1969 (Table 14).

Table 14. Federally Supported Indian Public Assistance Recipients, 1969

CATEGORY	CASES	PERSONS
Total	26,892	61,406
Aid to families with dependent children	12,356	45,957
Old age assistance	9,614	10,128
Aid to the permanently and totally disabled	4,303	4,649
Aid to the blind	619	672

Source: Bureau of Indian Affairs.

The enactment of the Nixon administration's Family Assistance Plan (FAP) could have dramatic effects for reservation residents. Assuming a guaranteed annual income of $1,600 for a family of four plus $300 for each additional dependent, the BIA estimated that two-thirds of the total number of cases and 88 percent of the number of individuals receiving general assistance from the Bureau in fiscal 1969 would have been eligible for the plan. Nearly 60 percent of BIA general-assistance expenditures were spent for these persons. It is estimated that if FAP had been in effect in

1960, Indian income would have been 72 percent higher than it actually was. As the median family income at that time was $1,800, the existence of FAP would have increased the median Indian income to $3,100.[5]

BUREAU OF INDIAN AFFAIRS WELFARE PROGRAM

While the type and amounts of assistance and services vary from reservation to reservation according to their economic conditions, resources, customs, and attitudes, the Bureau of Indian Affairs attempts to achieve some common goals among reservation residents. In general, the social services program aims to provide financial assistance to needy Indian families, counseling for those Indians with family or social problems, and welfare services for all dependent, neglected, and handicapped children.

Employing the budgetary standards of the state welfare agency of the state in which the individual or family lives to determine general-assistance needs, the BIA furnishes the assistance to meet living expenses or supplements available resources to bring income up to state standards. Cash or in-kind income received by applicants is subtracted from relief payments. In addition to the items provided in accordance with state standards, the BIA pays for burials, custodial care for adults in nursing homes, boarding homes, rest homes, or institutions, and clothing for school children when payment for these items is not otherwise available.

It has only been in recent years that the Bureau has been able to provide Indians with general assistance comparable to state schedules. The policy of the BIA Division of Social Services is that assistance should not be denied to eligible applicants even when it appears the funds in the budget for this purpose are exhausted. If this occurs, the BIA applies for supplementary funds from Congress. During the last five years, Congress has granted $12.7 million in supplemental welfare appropriations, $6 million of which was approved in fiscal 1970 alone.

The number of Indians receiving Bureau of Indian Affairs general-assistance payments has increased even more dramatically than categorical assistance. Over the past decade, the average monthly caseload has increased over threefold to 36,000 in 1970, and the amount spent has risen from $3.4 million in 1960 to $15.7 million in 1970 (Table 15).

Table 15. Welfare Programs

PROGRAM	AMOUNT (THOUSANDS)			PERSONS SERVED: AVERAGE MONTHLY CASELOAD		
	1960	1965	1970	1960	1965	1970
General assistance	$3,407	$6,031	$15,733	11,755	20,006	35,972
Child welfare						
Foster children	579	1,150	2,548	1,612	2,118	2,438
Institutional	207	462	1,546	277	421	704
Other	190	324	107	103	195	158
Social services only	⁂	⁂	⁂	9,790	12,298	14,942

⁂ Not applicable.
Source: Bureau of Indian Affairs.

Only Indians living on or near reservations and in jurisdictions under the Bureau of Indian Affairs in Alaska and Oklahoma are eligible for general assistance. Those for whom state, county, or local assistance is available are not eligible for Bureau assistance, but the BIA provides general assistance for individuals and families while their application for public assistance is pending and until they receive their first payment check. BIA social workers also help Indians file claims and appeal questionable adverse rulings, and they document reports to local agencies, state offices, and Bureau area offices to prevent discrimination against legitimate assistance claims. Any Indian eligible for public assistance who refuses to file an application or comply with the local agency's regulations is ineligible for BIA general assistance.

The BIA favors "workfare over welfare." Therefore, all applicants for, and adult recipients of, general assistance are expected to seek and accept available employment, including seasonal and off-reservation jobs if they have obtained such employment in the past, so long as the pay and working conditions are commensurate with prevailing practices in the community. Following general welfare practices, mothers with child care responsibilities are not forced to seek work, and heads of families are not forced to accept jobs away from home if the work will involve hardships or family disorganization.

TRIBAL WORK EXPERIENCE PROGRAM

In place of direct relief, the BIA has encouraged tribal councils to develop work programs that offer recipients an opportunity to perform useful work. These projects are modeled after the Work Experience and Training Program of the Economic Opportunity Act. Fifteen tribes operated fourteen work projects under contracts with the BIA in fiscal 1969 at an annual cost of $1 million. The extra costs accrued by the program are minimal since only heads of households eligible for general assistance participate in the program and participation is strictly voluntary on the part of the recipients. The Bureau of Indian Affairs pays the tribe the full assistance budget, including essential administrative costs, plus $30 a month for each worker to cover expenses incidental to the employment. Rather than receive a check from the Bureau, the worker then receives his regular allotment and additional $30 directly from the tribe.

Theoretically, the tribal councils administer their own programs, and they design the projects to suit their own needs so long as the recipients are not employed to displace regularly employed persons or used to fill vacancies in established positions and the project is not a commercially profit-making activity. The tribes are expected to bear or share the costs of administering the program, but funds from the general assistance account are provided when tribal resources are insufficient. Tribal contributions have actually been minimal, amounting to only $6,500 in fiscal 1969. Tools and materials are contributed by many different sources, including the U.S. Public Health Service, OEO programs, federal and public schools, community groups, and the workers themselves.

Some 1,200 heads of families receiving unduplicated general assistance participated in the Tribal Work Experience Program in 1969. Grants to tribes ranged from $1,600 to $455,000, and the most popular activities included the construction of recreational and sanitation facilities. The home improvement program and the Public Health Service cooperated with the construction and repair of several hundred homes on two reservations.

SOCIAL SERVICES AND CHILD WELFARE

In addition to providing relief to the poor for whom no other source of income is available, the BIA supports a number of other social services to its Indian clients. As in the case of cash income, the Bureau attempts not to duplicate state or local assistance available from welfare agencies, but to supplement the gaps between needs and existing assistance. BIA functions may range from advising an Indian about the availability of services in a state agency to providing counseling about family problems to offering diverse assistance to children in trouble and paying for their foster-home care. While BIA social services are offered to all Indians receiving general assistance or child-welfare assistance, it is not necessary for an individual or family to receive financial aid to be eligible for social services. A monthly average of 15,000 cases received only social services in 1970, an increase of some 5,000 over the past 10 years.

Child welfare is a major activity of BIA social-service agencies. When a social worker feels that a child is living in a home that is detrimental to his well-being, and if the child's parents are either absent or unwilling to improve the home environment, the worker must refer the case to either the appropriate state agency or tribal authority. If a child on a reservation is not in the custody of his parents, BIA social workers can either refer his case to the responsible agency, offer assistance to the persons caring for the child, or help the child's relatives obtain legal custody or guardianship. If the child is subject to abuse or neglect, however, the worker may take action to refer the child to a court. Bureau caseworkers can initiate court action only in the absence of federal, state, and tribal organizations with authority and when friends and relatives willing to take such action on behalf of the child are lacking.

Because the BIA social-services policy is to keep children with their own parents whenever possible, a program of assistance to the child in his own home is given primary emphasis. Children whose parents are either unwilling or unable to care for them can be placed in foster-family homes, specialized institutions treating the deaf, blind, mentally retarded, and delinquent, or in federal boarding or mission schools. Although the latter are presumably used for children who will profit from group living and those who require placement due to a temporary problem in their family life, boarding schools are also used as "foster homes" when no family can be found to care for a child. As most foster families seem to prefer infants and very young children, many of the older children find themselves being cared for in a boarding school the entire year. All foster placements must be requested by the natural parents or demanded by court action to sever the child from a debilitating home environment.

The Bureau of Indian Affairs spent $4.2 million for child welfare in fiscal 1970, an increase of more than threefold over the past decade. Of the total amount expended, about $2.5 million was spent for foster care and $1.5 million for institutional care. It might be noted that the average monthly cost per child for foster home care and institutional care has risen from $41 in 1960 to $108 in 1970. As the BIA policy is to follow state standards, average monthly costs per child vary from less than $100 to several hundred, the smaller amounts usually being used for unspecialized institutional care and the larger amounts for intensive training for the blind and the deaf.

The BIA employs 219 professional social workers. Their average caseload is 140, ranging from 41 for the social workers for the Shawnees in Oklahoma to 281 for those serving the Standing Rock Sioux Agency in North Dakota. The average caseload of BIA social workers is double the standard caseload suggested by most social-work authorities. As the number of Indians served by the Bureau's social-welfare program has been increasing each year, it is likely that the average case responsibility will increase in the years ahead.

Several tribes have their own welfare programs to supplement state and local welfare programs. Nearly all tribes have a burial program that allots funds for the costs of burials without regard to need, but this is the only element of many tribal programs.

The Navajos have the most extensive welfare program, including such components as clothing for school children, the distribution of surplus commodities, a scholarship program, maintenance of burial grounds, and a public works program. The cost of the school clothing provision is about $1.5 million annually and is distributed among the 97 chapter houses for local councilmen to distribute among their own communities.

TRIBAL TRUST FUNDS

One of the most significant consequences of poverty is that it produces diverse obstacles the poor must overcome before they are able to help themselves. Still, these difficulties are surmountable, and bootstrap operations have often been successful. Some poor communities and nations have tightened their collective belts to ensure a better social and economic future for their people. For example, Puerto Rico, whose average per capita income before World War II was no better than on reservations, has expanded its economy over the past two decades through the investment of federal contributions accumulated during the war.

Although the economic situation of America's Indians is by no means identical to that of Puerto Rico following the Second World War, it is clear that Indian tribes can also stimulate economic growth and social development by investing whatever savings they can salvage into reservation projects. Some Indian tribes have substantial resources and savings, and it is not at all certain that they are moving as rapidly as they could toward economic and community development. Certainly government and outside private funds could be more effectively utilized for these purposes, but experience has indicated that the impetus for increased development must come from the involved population. The history of the federal government's ineffectiveness in leading reservation Indians toward greater self-reliance makes it obvious that Indians will have to assume a greater responsibility for the development of their own economies and increasingly invest their admittedly limited resources in self-improvement efforts.

By the end of 1970, tribes had accumulated about $396 million in trust funds from the lease and development of mineral, oil, and other resources, judgment awards of claims against the federal government, and tribal industries. It is estimated that from 60 to 70 percent of earnings on mineral deposits is generally paid to individual tribal members rather than invested for future development.[6] Similarly, much of the money awarded from the settlement of claims is distributed among members of the tribe. Between 1951 and 1964, for instance, approximately $42 million of a total of $102 million, or 41 percent, was shared among tribal members.[7]

Few would disagree that Indians need more income for immediate consumption, and experience in recent years has indicated that tribal establishments assign a higher priority to income maintenance than to long-term development. Existing trust funds, however, could provide the seed capital necessary to finance programs created and administered by tribal organizations with a minimum of interference by federal officials.

DEVELOPMENT OF TRIBAL TRUST FUNDS

The trust-fund policy dates back to an 1819 treaty with the Cherokee tribe. Some trust funds were created when the federal government forced Indians to move from their homes and rewarded the more agreeable migrants with a specific sum to be held in their tribe's name. Other funds were the result of the sale of tribal land to the United States either through negotiation or through force, when tribal consent was not obtained. The government deposited the receipts in the United States Treasury for the "benefit" of the displaced tribes.

Until recently, nearly all tribal trust money was deposited in the Treasury, where it earned an annual interest rate of 4 percent. In July 1966, however, the Bureau of Indian Affairs approved a program to increase the rate of return on tribal funds by investing in government securities and bank certificates of deposit that are secured by either commercial collateral or bond. While the decision to invest tribal trust funds or keep them in the Treasury is not governed by explicit regulations, the BIA generally makes the decision to withdraw funds from the Treasury for deposit in banks or investment in securities and then obtains permission from the tribes. BIA investors attempt to deposit the money where it will earn the highest rates of interest, so funds are often placed in accounts with banks far from the reservation. In most cases, however, BIA officials will try to convince local banks to match the country's highest obtainable rates of interest so tribes can have their funds in nearby banks without sacrificing valuable interest.

The $396 million in tribal trust funds at the end of 1970 was distributed as follows: $35 million was held in the United States Treasury; $250 million was deposited in banks; and $111 million was invested in securities. The investment brought a total return of $26 million to the tribal treasuries.

In addition, the transfer of most trust funds from the Treasury will probably be followed by further investments in common stocks and bonds. The Navajos have already established a $10 million educational fund from money invested in corporate stocks and mutual funds. The increasing financial sophistication of some tribes accompanied by the growing flexibility of the Bureau of Indian Affairs (which holds veto power over the transfer of trust funds) may make this investment procedure more common and profitable for other tribes. Because the purchase of common stocks requires professional expertise, only those tribes with adequate resources can afford such an investment. There are, however, at least 15 tribes with assets exceeding $5 million that could afford expert investment counsel.

Not included as tribal trust monies are local tribal funds. These are the funds held in the treasuries of tribes organized under the Indian Reorganization Act of 1934, monies a tribe earns either from its own members or from third parties without any intervention by the federal government, and finances granted local tribes from the U.S. Treasury by acts of Congress. As federal administrative authorities do not claim control over the disposition of these funds unless such power is specifically provided under tribal constitutions, charters, loan trust or other legal agreements, the BIA does not maintain a record of funds held in local tribal funds.

SOURCES OF TRUST FUNDS

The two major sources of tribal trust funds in recent years have been earnings received from the deposits of oil, gas, and other minerals found on Indian reservations and from the settlement of claims before the Indian Claims Commission. Indian trust funds increased from a modest $4.5 million in 1840 to $28.5 million in 1947 and soared to nearly $400 million in the next 23 years.

Income from gas, oil, and other minerals has bulged the trust fund accounts of a few lucky and business-wise tribes. While a few tribes enjoy most of the income from natural resources, experts believe that still many more tribes stand to gain from oil, gas, and mineral operations. For instance, gas and/or oil deposits have been found on the Hopi, Northern Cheyenne, Standing Rock Sioux, Apache, and Seminole and Miccosuke reservations. Tribes expected to increase their earnings from mineral deposits include the Zuñis, the Northern Cheyennes, and the Indians on the Uintah and Ouray reservation. (Income from natural resources is discussed in Chapter 5.)

In 1946, Congress established the Indian Claims Commission to process the monetary grievances of Indian tribes against the United States government.[8] The Commission was part of the termination approach that gained momentum in the 1950s; proponents of the act anticipated that compensation paid to tribes with legitimate claims would help them become economically independent. The intent of Congress was that the awards be earmarked for programs that would help develop the infrastructure on reservations and reduce tribal dependence upon the federal government.

Awards had been made to tribes before the establishment of the Indian Claims Commission. In 1938, for example, Congress appropriated $4.4 million to the Shoshones to compensate for the hardships incurred when the Arapahoes were moved to the Shoshone reservation, and the Klamaths won a claim for $5.3 million for tribal land the federal government had given to the state of Oregon. But the Indian Claims Commission grants awards not only for mistakes, frauds, and blatant wrongdoings; it also allows for "claims based upon fair and honorable dealings that are not recognized by any existing rule or law of equity." Consequently, the Otoe and Missouri tribes were granted $1.7 million in 1955 for the loss of land they occupied without official title. Most of the claims have been concerned, however, with land either forcibly taken from Indians or for which insufficient prices were paid.

While the original act dictated that all claims filed by 1951 be adjudicated within ten years, the great number and complexity of cases and cumbersome bureaucratic procedures common in all dealings with Indians made it necessary to extend the Commission until April, 1972. All claims were filed by August 13, 1951, and the original 370 petitions were subsequently divided into 606 separate dockets. By mid-1969, the Indian Claims Commission had approved 150 cases for $305 million, had dismissed 154 cases, and had 302 cases in various stages of judicial proceedings (Table 16).

Table 16. Dockets Completed by the Indian Claims
Commission through Fiscal 1969

FISCAL YEAR	NUMBER OF DOCKETS COMPLETED		TOTAL AMOUNT OF AWARDS (MILLIONS)	CUMULATIVE AWARDS (MILLIONS)
	DISMISSALS	AWARDS		
Total	154	150		
1947–59	88	17	$20.4	$ 20.4
1960	7	13	21.6	42.0
1961	5	5	14.9	56.9
1962	4	2	18.1	75.0
1963	9	8	18.3	93.3
1964	7	9	15.8	109.1
1965	7	26	55.4	164.5
1966	2	12	38.7	203.2
1967	2	7	21.5	224.7
1968	3	23	43.6	268.3
1969	20	28	36.9	305.2

Source: Indian Claims Commission, 1969 Annual Report.

Once the Indian Claims Commission awards an uncontested claim, Congress automatically appropriates the total amount of the award. It is then the responsibility of the BIA to determine the beneficiaries of the award, which is usually made to the aggrieved entity at the historical time of the wrongdoing. The process of identifying the beneficiaries is often difficult and lengthy. The recipient of a claims award can be a tribe that is no longer a cohesive entity, whose members have long since dispersed, or whose members have never been an organized group. For instance, a claims award was recently granted to the Southern Paiute Nation. Upon investigation, the BIA found that there is no tribal group today known by that name; that even historically the tribe was a small and scattered group; and that this title has never been used in official treaties.

The Bureau studies the current socioeconomic situation of the tribe and its members both on and off the reservation. The nature of the modern organization is thoroughly investigated, and a roll of awardees is ordinarily prepared. If the award is intended for current members of an organized tribal entity, the preparation of the roll is a simple matter. If, however, the award requires a descendancy roll, the process of verifying the list of legal claimants is complex, costly, and time-consuming. The final roll of award recipients requires verification by the Secretary of the Interior and congressional action.

The BIA has generally found that it is not feasible to persuade tribes to invest their awarded claims in programs designed to improve the reservation infrastructures. In many cases, legal beneficiaries who live off the reservation have pressured the BIA to propose and Congress to approve the distribution of awards among individual claimants rather than to make a lump-sum award to the tribe. In other instances, the tribes have decided to distribute all or part of their funds among their members rather than use the money for tribal programs.

By February 1970, the BIA had disbursed $148.9 million of the awarded money. About a third of this total was disbursed under per capita legislation, and the rest was granted to tribal entities. But of the $100.6 million given to the tribes, only $38.5 million was actually programmed for tribal projects, including scholarship awards, community-development efforts, tribal business enterprises, manpower programs, and construction of social-service facilities.[9]

As the nearly 1 to 1 ratio of awards to dismissals clearly indicates, all tribes that believed they were entitled to retribution did not receive favorable settlements. And many other small and poor tribes didn't file claims because they lacked the financial resources or political clout to obtain initial congressional approval to process a claim. Lawyers were initially reluctant to represent the smaller tribes because of the highly specialized knowledge this type of litigation requires and the uncertainty of collecting fees. But a few attorneys who became expert in Indian claims have reaped substantial rewards from the 10 percent of net judgments and court costs earned from each case.

Some tribes had difficulties in other areas. They had to spend time and money to establish grounds for suit, the identity of the petitioners, the presentation of specific evidence, and an appropriate basis for the assessment of land values. These processes involved the services of experts to examine records, conduct archaeological investigations, and compile ethnographic and other documentary materials. In 1963, Congress established a revolving loan fund of $900,-000, increased to $1,800,000 in 1966, to assist tribes in the engagement of technicians to aid claims attorneys in the preparation of their law suits.

The Claims Commission has achieved some of its original aims but has failed miserably on many accounts. The Commission was established to expedite the settling of claims, but it has proceeded as slowly as the Court of Claims previously hearing all Indian complaints. It has continued to function as a court, employing the same time-consuming procedures that frustrated both the claimants and Congress. In the words of one commissioner, ". . . the Indian Claims Commission has failed throughout the time of its existence to exercise the initiative in hearing and determining the claims before it."[10]

THE POTENTIAL OF TRIBAL TRUST FUNDS

Many of the reasons why Indian tribes have not been able to invest substantial amounts in economic and community development are obvious. Their immediate needs are so pressing that even resources allocated to income maintenance instead of tribal programs are insufficient to appreciably affect the individual Indian's standard of living. Funds from claims awards have been dispersed slowly and inefficiently, and until recently trust funds have not been invested where they could earn the highest rates of interest without violating prudent investment practices.

The claims of off-reservation Indians to tribal resources are legitimate but have too frequently forced per capita disbursement in lieu of tribal investment. While nonresident tribal members should share in profits, they should not be permitted to erode principal investments. Interest on tribal investments could be shared among all tribal members without affecting the capital, much the same as interest is shared among stockholders, without dissipating the principal investment in a corporation.

The object of federal policy should be to minimize the risk of and provide incentives for developmental investment. To the degree that economic and social development is likely to succeed, guarantees of return will have a low overall cost. Certainly, there is as much or more reason to ensure tribal investments as there is to ensure loans made by outside sources as is currently being proposed. It is additionally worthwhile to subsidize tribal investments where they will be a substitute for federal outlays or where they will result in improvements that reduce federal responsibilities and help develop Indian communities.

These approaches could be implemented along traditional lines. The government could guarantee loans made by the tribes to their own economic-development bodies, which could be established as separate nonprofit groups patterned after those now operating in urban ghettos. Representatives could be elected and/or appointed, but the structure of these bodies should maximize their independence so they could pursue chiefly economic goals. Loans with federal guarantees from outsiders could also be directed to these groups. Seed money could be provided on a matching basis by the government and the tribe, perhaps with the sale of shares to individual members as well as with contributions from tribal funds.

More generally, matching grants or loans could be used to induce the tribes to invest in their own future. For instance, for each dollar invested in social overhead capital, the government could add an extra dollar. By establishing different matching formulas for different investments, tribal investments could be coaxed into desired channels without direct federal control.

If such measures could be implemented, they would accomplish significant goals. They would draw additional resources into the development of the reservation infrastructure and give the tribes more control over their own affairs. Moreover, they would probably improve the general economic and social well-being of the reservations.

NOTES

1. Act of March 3, 1885, 23 Stat. 385.

2. Act of March 4, 1909, 35 Stat. 1088.

3. Felix Cohen, "Indian Rights and the Federal Courts," *Minnesota Law Review,* January 1940.

4. William A. Brophy and Sophie D. Aberle, *The Indian: America's Unfinished Business,* University of Oklahoma Press, Norman, 1966, p. 52.

5. Alan Sorkin, "Poverty and Dropouts: The Case of the American Indian," *Growth and Change,* July 1970, p. 16.

6. Alan Sorkin, "Indian Trust Funds," *Toward Economic Development for Native American Communities,* Joint Economic Committee, 91st Cong., 1st Sess., 1969, vol. 2, p. 451.

7. Computed from Robert Pennington, "Summary of Indian Claims Commission Dockets," unpublished memorandum, January 1968, p. 2.

8. Pub. L. No. 79-726, Aug. 13, 1946.

9. Bureau of Indian Affairs, "Summary of Indian Claims Commission Dockets," unpublished memorandum, Feb. 2, 1970.

10. John T. Vance, "The Congressional Mandate and the Indian Claims Commission," *North Dakota Law Review,* Spring 1969, p. 335.

"WE THANK HIM THAT HE HAS GIVEN US THE EARTH, OUR MOTHER FROM WHOSE BREAST ALL THINGS GROW."—SENECA PRAYER

Chapter 5

The Development
of Natural Resources

THE IMPORTANCE OF NATURAL RESOURCES

Indians hold title or claim to vast tracts of land and many valuable natural resources that are not only a primary source of employment and earnings, but also the only form of wealth that Indians usually possess. Indian lands and their use are subject to BIA jurisdiction. At the end of 1969, there were 55.4 million acres, including 39.6 million which were tribally owned, 10.7 million which were allotted to individuals, and 5.1 million of government-owned land which were reserved for Indian use. This vast acreage served many productive purposes and was used both directly by Indians and by outsiders paying rent to the tribes or to individual Indians (Table 17).

Income from these lands is substantial. Surface leasing, permitting, and stumpage payments for the use of Indian lands by non-Indians generated $70.4 million in 1969 (Table 18). Indian users paid $17.9 million essentially in transfer payments to tribes for the use of their land. Many also produced goods on the lands they either owned or used without payment, benefiting from an imputed rent of more than

Top: *Ute Mountain reservation, Towaoc, Colorado. Measuring irrigation water for efficient use.* Bottom: *Logging in the state of Washington.*

Table 17. Uses of Indian Lands, 1969

	ACRES (THOUSANDS)	PERCENT OF TOTAL
Total	55,750*	100
Open grazing	33,971	61
Noncommercial timber	8,821	16
Commercial timber	5,475	10
Oil and gas	3,483	6
Dry farm	1,832	3
Other minerals	940	2
Irrigation	650	1
Other uses	479	1
Business	99	—

* The figures on land ownership and land use are prepared independently and differ slightly.

Source: BIA, Land Use Inventory and Production Record, Report 50-1.

$25 million. In addition, many private jobs on or near reservations are involved in the use of their natural resources, and these jobs account for a substantial portion of aggregate Indian wage earnings. The land holdings of Indians and the resources they contain are basic to their economic life.

Unfortunately, the land-based resources of the Indians are underproductive, being overutilized in some areas and underutilized in most others. For a variety of reasons, including Indian antipathy to the exploitation of their lands and BIA apathy in advocating Indians' rights and needs,

Table 18. Cash Revenue from Property Leases to Non-Indians, 1969

	REVENUE (THOUSANDS)	PERCENT OF TOTAL
Total	$70,439	100
Forestry	23,074	33
Oil and gas	22,445	32
Farm and pasture	13,826	20
Other mineral	3,992	6
Business	3,493	5
Grazing	1,967	3
Outdoor recreation	728	1
Other surface	914	1

Source: BIA, Land Use Inventory and Production Record, Report 50-1.

they are receiving nowhere near the income and employment their resource endowments could provide. BIA technicians have estimated that through proper utilization, the
contribution to the personal income could be increased from
$66.9 million in 1968 to a projected $122.0 million in 1975,
an increase of more than four-fifths.[1] Whatever the accuracy
of these estimates, it is clear that Indian resources can and
should be even more important in the future, though overall
economic development on or near reservations may reduce
the Indians' relative dependence on their land resources.

FARMING AND RANCHING

The largest proportion of Indian lands are used for agricultural purposes. Grazing takes place on the least productive
lands, requiring vast areas and paying the lowest per acre
rents; dry farming is more productive, returning moderate
rents; irrigated farming is very intensive and yields a high
income per acre. In 1969, dry farming was carried out on
1,832,000 acres, and there were an estimated 613,000
acres irrigated. More than two-thirds of the remaining area,
or almost 34 million acres, supported open grazing, and an
additional 11 million acres of timberland were also used
for grazing purposes. The agricultural lands allotted to
individuals are generally the most productive. Over four-
fifths of dry farm land is individually owned, and more than
half of the irrigated acres. The tribes own the less valuable
or at least the less developed lands accounting for nearly
three-fourths of the acreage devoted to open grazing.
Government lands are not important in the aggregate for
farming and ranching operations.

INCOME

The value of agricultural lands varies widely from reservation to reservation, as do average farm and ranch earnings

and rental receipts. For instance, grazing lands rented for 35 cents an acre on the San Juan Pueblo reservation in New Mexico during fiscal 1960, while irrigated farm lands went for $20 per acre on the Gila River reservation in Arizona. Grazing lands averaged $3.82 for all agricultural rentals. Reservations differ in the quantity as well as the quality of their land, especially on a per capita basis. But agricultural resources are more evenly distributed than timber, oil and gas, or other minerals, and they are an important source of employment and income on most reservations.

The agricultural use of reservation lands by non-Indians provides substantial income to the tribes and their members. In 1969, farm and pasture rentals paid by non-Indians generated $13.8 million in income, while grazing permits to outsiders added an extra $2.0 million. More significantly, an estimated 27,500 Indian families, or almost one of every three, operated an agricultural enterprise in 1969, though only 5,581 of these families were earning more than half of their income through agriculture and were able to maintain an "adequate" standard of living. Of all Indian families operating agricultural enterprises, 23 percent were raising cash crops alone, 46 percent were raising livestock alone, and the remainder were involved in a combination of farming and ranching or some other type of agricultural enterprise. It has often been claimed that Indians, with the exception of a few tribes, are not inclined towards farming and have a definite preference for ranching.

Indian farmers and ranchers raised products valued at $53.9 million in 1969 on lands which they owned and an additional $31.6 million on those leased from other Indians. A rule of thumb in agricultural operations is that the value of the output is usually divided in three equal shares for operating costs, rent, and the entrepreneur. If this held true on reservations, Indians using their own lands would be benefiting from an imputed rent of $18.0 million, and Indian farm and ranch operators would be earning profits and imputed wages of $28.5 million. In addition, a large share of the required farm and ranch workers (as opposed to operators) are Indians. In 1969, there were an estimated 8,329 full-time and 28,024 part-time jobs in agriculture on Indian lands,[2] with 8,719 and 23,563 respectively in related businesses. Indians probably held a majority of these jobs with a subsequently significant wage revenue. Whatever the case, farming and ranching are of undisputed importance to the reservation economies.

FEDERAL PROGRAMS

The BIA has several programs for assisting Indian farmers and ranchers, for improving Indian lands, and for increasing their yield. Additionally, the United States Department of Agriculture (USDA) provides several services which are available to Indians, though it operates no exclusively Indian programs. The 1970 appropriations for the BIA programs and the estimated allocations to Indians under the USDA's programs amounted to more than $27 million (Table 19).

Table 19. Appropriations for Agricultural Purposes Directed to Indians, Fiscal 1970

Total	$27.3
BIA appropriations	17.8
Rangelands	2.0
Fire suppression	0.1
Agricultural extension	2.2
Soil and moisture conservation	6.0
Irrigation operation and maintenance	1.4
Construction of irrigation systems	6.0
Department of Agriculture	9.5
Farmers Home Administration	3.5
Agricultural Stabilization and Conservation	3.9
Rural Electrification Administration	1.5
Soil Conservation Service	0.6

Note: Details do not necessarily add to total because of rounding.
Source: U.S. Office of Management and Budget.

Most of the BIA's programs focus on providing technical assistance of various types and are short on funds for project development. The rangeland program, with an annual budget of almost $2 million, is devoted to management, planning and counseling for ranching operations. In recent years, this program has been applied vigorously to help Indians get the full appraised value for the use of their grazing lands and to encourage them to use these lands themselves. This has had notable success, with grazing permits to outsiders increasing from 44 cents to 55 cents per acre between 1966 and 1969, while the number of acres grazed by non-Indians was reduced from 4.1 to 3.6 million acres. The BIA's Counseling and Agricultural Extension Service is funded for another $2 million annually, and its extension agents give training in home economics and run the Indian 4-H program. While the 4-H program served an estimated 14,000 Indian youths in 1969, it focuses on community development and does not directly increase agricultural productivity. The most significant BIA technical assistance effort is its Soil and Moisture Conservation (SMC) program, which funds roughly 380 professional and subprofessional positions. About a third of the persons filling these slots are Indian aides, and the rest are trained technicians. These advisors organize meetings, give individual counseling, and provide the technical groundwork for soil and moisture conservation improvements. Most of the $6 million SMC budget is spent for this technical assistance, with less than 10 percent of funds being used for capital outlays. Investments in physical improvements come chiefly from the land users, who "voluntarily" cooperate with the program. Cooperators spent an estimated $36.5 million in 1969 for such measures as brush and pest control, strip cropping, canals and ditches, terraces, and tree planting. Non-Indians are more active participants because their cooperation is generally required by their leases. Three-fourths of their rangelands and four-fifths of their farmlands are in satisfactory compliance with SMC plans, compared with three-fifths and 54 percent, respectively, of Indian-operated lands.

The operation, repair, and maintenance of Indian irrigation systems are primarily financed from direct charges to users of irrigated land. When Indians are unable to pay such charges, the BIA supplements their contribution. The supplements cost an estimated $1.4 million in fiscal 1970. There were 650,000 acres of irrigable tribal, allotted, and government lands at the end of 1969. During that year, the value of output per acre was almost twice that on lands used for dry farming. In order to increase the number of irrigated acres, $6.0 million was budgeted in fiscal 1970 for construction, $1.4 million of which went to the large Navajo Indian Irrigation Project.

Although funds under the USDA programs are not set aside for Indians, some estimates have been made of the value of the services they receive. Under the Farmers Home Administration loan programs in fiscal 1970, an estimated $3.5 million in credit (mostly at subsidized interest rates) was extended for farm improvements and operations, home purchases, and other purposes. The Agricultural Stabilization and Conservation Service expended $3.9 million in fiscal 1970, mostly for price support payments or cost-sharing on Indian conservation investments; and the Soil Conservation Service spent an additional $0.6 million to provide technical assistance on conservation practices. Also, the Rural Electrification Administration spent $1.5 million to cover the costs above repayment of providing electrical power to reservations, while the USDA's Consumer and Marketing Service allocated $2.4 million in fiscal 1970 almost entirely for food stamps and direct food distribution.

Despite these various forms of aid, Indians still receive a disproportionately small share of the federal assistance funds for farmers and ranchers. According to the BIA, the overall government expenditure on privately owned non-reservation land is still about 2.4 times the amount spent per acre on Indian lands. Since most Indians have a low income, they lack the resources needed to make their operations efficient. For instance, only 16 million acres of the land used by Indians for agricultural purposes are judged to have a high level of production. Obviously, the vast majority of Indian agricultural lands are not fully productive.

There have been some recent improvements in the farming, ranching, and agricultural leasing operations on Indian lands. While federal agencies can claim a large share of the credit for the increase of more than a third in the value of total agricultural production by Indians, some of the gains are accounted for by price increases. Nevertheless, the greater productivity of non-Indian farmers and ranchers using Indian lands indicates both that Indian agricultural techniques are relatively underdeveloped and that Indians are leasing their best lands. The wide divergence between the outputs per acre in operations run by Indians and those operated by non-Indians is clear (Table 20).

OBSTACLES TO INCREASED AGRICULTURAL PRODUCTIVITY

If Indians are to increase their own agricultural productivity, they will need more resources to improve their land and acquire equipment. Of equal importance is the need for training in agricultural technology. Increased resources and training will not be sufficient, however, for three major obstacles will have to be overcome: the heirship problem, which complicates the ownership and management of Indian lands and leads to their irrational utilization; the challenge of deciding what to do with the "excess" families now engaged in inefficient agricultural operations; and the lack of irrigation systems needed to implement modern methods of farming and ranching.

Table 20. *Agricultural Production on Indian Lands, 1969*

	INDIAN OPERATED			NON-INDIAN OPERATED		
	ACREAGE (THOU- SANDS)	VALUE (THOU- SANDS)	VALUE PER ACRE	ACREAGE (THOU- SANDS)	VALUE (THOU- SANDS)	VALUE PER ACRE
Cultivated row crop	59.5	$ 5,743.6	$96.53	281.0	$53,826.7	$191.55
Small grains	200.9	7,187.8	35.78	638.8	27,511.0	43.06
Forage hay	243.5	9,272.2	38.08	301.3	15,162.5	50.32
Horticulture and garden	22.8	5,272.4	23.12	16.8	12,324.4	73.36
Grazing	36,342.2	51,258.3	1.58	6,283.5	36,496.6	5.81

Source: Bureau of Indian Affairs.

The heirship problem is a result of the federal trust held over Indian lands. Upon the death of the original owner of an allotted estate, its title is held in trust for all heirs. The federal government does not have the legal authority to assign this property to a sole owner, and there are several reasons why the heirs do not settle the estate in the usual fashion of deciding upon a single owner. Typically, any single heir lacks the cash or credit to purchase the rights of others; there is little incentive to purchase the rights since the government bears the cost and responsibility of administering the trust estate; and Indian families prefer familial ownership. As a result, many heirs hold a fraction of the title to some tracts, and the problem is compounded with each death and redivision of title. A 1965 BIA survey found that only 40 percent of total allotted tracts had a single owner while 17 percent had 11 or more owners. In 1960, half of the 12.9 million allotted acres had heirship status.[3]

A sizable proportion of this heirship land is not productive because the numerous heirs cannot agree upon its use. Any single heir can move onto a tract and prevent all other uses except heir residence. Where no claims are made, the reservation superintendent can rent heirship lands for the purpose he deems most productive. Thus, in 1960, 541,000 of the 6,176,000 total heirship acres served no productive purpose, including 69,700 of the 211,300 acres of irrigated land.

Much of the remaining allotted land — not in heirship status — is divided into small tracts where single ownership has been maintained by physical subdivision. In 1960, single-owner allotments averaged only 180 acres, an area generally too small for efficient farm operations.

Though only a fifth of Indian lands are individually owned and only half of the one-owner lands are in heirship status, these lands are usually the most potentially productive. For instance, in 1969 there were 40.1 million acres of tribal land compared with 10.6 million acres of allotted land. But the tribes had only 272,500 acres of irrigated land as opposed to 338,000 owned individually; there were only 288,800 acres of tribal dry farm land compared with 1.51 million allotted acres. Most tribal land is used for open grazing because it is not suited for other purposes.

The problem is not only that valuable allotted tracts are often too small for efficient use and that those in heirship status are sometimes not used at all, but also that these tracts are often in the middle of tribal lands and restrict the efficient use of larger tracts. Many tribes have initiated land consolidation programs to buy back allotted tracts and consolidate their holdings. For instance, tribal lands have increased from 39.5 million acres in 1966 to 40.1 million acres in 1969, while individual lands have decreased from 11.0 million acres to 10.6 million. Several plans have been suggested to eliminate the heirship problem, such as the automatic reversion of title to the tribe when the number of heirs is too great, and the collection of administrative fees on heirship lands to encourage heirs to reach a settlement. But these and other proposals have not been accepted, and tribal purchases are not helping to solve the problem. Expanded efforts should be undertaken to alleviate the heirship problem and to promote operations on an efficient scale.

If Indian lands could be reallocated so that all farming and ranching tracts were of an optimum size, there would be the problem of the excess families now underemployed in small operations. The "agricultural revolution" has been late in reaching the reservations, but indications are that its effects may be even more serious than in other rural areas. Indians are often deeply rooted in their land and highly immobile; they seem to continue their operations even though they are unprofitable. Thus, the number of Indian families operating agricultural enterprises actually increased from 1966 to 1969, despite a decrease in the number who were judged by BIA field personnel to be adequately supported on more than a half-time basis from these pursuits. The number of part-time operators—those with an adequate income but working less than half-time at farming or ranching—increased slightly, while the number working full- or part-time in agriculture but earning a less than "adequate" income rose even more dramatically. In other words, there is an increasing number of Indians who conduct unprofitable agricultural operations. Efforts to increase the number of profitable enterprises cannot neglect the marginal farmers and ranchers who will require employment and training in some productive occupation.

However, jobs could be provided in agriculture and most of these families could continue in farming and ranching if Indians increased the use of their own lands and were trained and assisted to become efficient operators. The BIA estimates that if the present agricultural acreage were subdivided into efficient sizes for the various types of operations and if only Indians were involved in their farming or ranching, 60,000 families could be supported adequately as farm or ranch operators. The number compares favorably with the 5,581 earning a reasonable income on more than a half-time basis in 1969. Certainly the 20,000 marginal and part-time farming and ranching families could be absorbed if the Indians used their lands more effectively.

Not only are non-Indians renting the most productive

lands, but their rental payments are probably less than
market value. In 1969, non-Indians produced goods valued
at $109.3 million on Indian farm and pasture lands and paid
only $13.8 million in rents. This amounts to about an eighth
of the value of output, rather than the one-third proportion
estimated by the rule of thumb prevailing for the rental of
non-Indian lands. Some of this is justified because the renters
pay in advance or assist Indians when they are in need, and
there are instances where Indians have chosen to keep old
renters rather than accept higher cash offers. Also, non-
Indian operators are required by their leases to make certain
improvements. Despite BIA claims to the contrary, it is
doubtful that these factors make up for the low percentage
of farm output paid in rent. The BIA has recommended that
Indians contract for crop shares rather than cash payments,
so that rentals could be tied more explicitly to the output
of the rented land. This would be a good idea if the BIA
would take adequate steps to write and enforce such contracts. Rentals could be increased on Indian lands as much
as $5 to $10 million if the tribes and their members would
demand the most for their land and if the BIA would increase
its efforts to provide the counsel and control to insure maximum rental fees.

One area of improvement is especially fraught with
controversy—the increase of irrigated Indian lands. By any
measure, irrigated lands are more productive than those
which are not irrigated. In the arid and semiarid regions of
the Western United States, water is one of the most vital
resources, and much of the land on Indian reservations can
only become agriculturally productive through extensive
irrigation.

Though Indian lands are extremely well situated with
respect to water sources, only 436,518 acres were publicly,
and 176,168 privately, irrigated in 1969. There is little
doubt that Indian lands have not been as equally developed

as other lands in the same states. For instance, reservations in Arizona had 132,790 irrigated acres, or less than a tenth of the irrigated acreage in the state, even though reservations account for over a fifth of Arizona's land area.

The failure to irrigate Indian lands is largely due to opposition from other non-Indian water users and to indefensible tendencies of the BIA to promote its own best interest. This is well illustrated by the case of the Navajo Indian Irrigation Project, a designated $175 to $200 million effort to provide water for a large area of San Juan County, New Mexico. This project began at the same time as a companion program of the same magnitude for nonreservation lands, but progress was so slow that it was only 18 percent finished by the time the non-Indian project was 90 percent completed. The proposed budget for fiscal 1971 would have cut off all funds for the Navajo project, and Congress supplied $4 million only after a public uproar. The scheduled expenditures, however, are $15 million per year. One reason for the limited funding is the low priority given to irrigation, but another is undoubtedly pressure from influential representatives of the neighboring areas that demand the water for their own uses.

The Navajo case is only one, and certainly not the most flagrant, example of the many ways in which Indians' rights to valuable water resources have been bypassed or left undeveloped. In the "Winters Doctrine" enunciated by the Supreme Court in 1906, Indian rights to the use of neighboring water sources for the irrigation of their land were clearly indicated.[4] Nevertheless, there exist numerous instances where federal agencies have curtailed or limited Indian water supplies. The excuse offered has usually been that Indians do not need the water because they do not have any immediate uses — but they do not have any immediate uses because irrigation expenditures have been limited. Here, perhaps more than anywhere else in the management of Indian resources, the federal government has failed to live up to its trust responsibility. The BIA has been lax in its advocacy of Indian water rights and has been unable to get money for irrigation projects. The interests of non-Indian areas have prevailed in the Department of Interior's efforts. More Indian lands could and should be profitably irrigated, and adequate water supplies must be guaranteed so that agricultural and industrial development can be effected in the future.

But even without irrigation, there are ways in which the use of Indian lands for agricultural purposes can be improved. The striking increases in the output by Indian farmers and ranchers and in the rental return on Indian agricultural lands between 1966 and 1967 are indicative of the gains which can still be made. All too often, agricultural programs are dismissed simply because agriculture is nationally declining in importance. But there is no reason to believe that investment in this area would have a smaller return than investment in any other natural resource. In all likelihood, it would be much more productive because of the greater human resources involved in agriculture. Agricultural improvements would have a much more widespread effect than would increased income from other uses of Indian lands.

FORESTRY

Approximately 5.5 million acres, or one-ninth of all reservation lands, contain commercially valuable timber. Timber provides substantial income and employment for many tribes and their members. "Stumpage payments" for timber harvesting privileges yield more cash income than the lease of any other reservation resource, except oil and gas. And in 1969, with the prevailing high prices for lumber, stumpage receipts rose to $23.1 million, which exceeded the $22.4 million revenues from oil and gas leases. Many jobs were also provided for Indians in logging, timber processing, and related industries. These activities accounted for an estimated 3,320 man-years of direct and indirect Indian employment in 1968 as well as a wage bill estimated at $15.9 million.[5] In addition, forests and the lakes and streams within them attract a large number of tourists for outdoor recreational purposes. The estimated 10 million visitor-days related to the use of Indian lands and forests generated $3.1 million in tribal income in 1968. Many of the visitors depended upon the recreational facilities constructed and available on the reservations, but most were attracted by the natural resources themselves.

Like other resources, valuable forest reserves are unevenly distributed, and a few reservations receive the majority of stumpage payments and benefit from the bulk of employment opportunities. Seven reservations contain 55 percent of the total commercial forest acreage; they received 88 percent of total stumpage payments in 1968, and they had 65 percent of the estimated Indian jobs in forestry-related industries. Seven other tribes account for most of the remaining income and employment, with the fourteen together receiving 96 percent of all stumpage payments and accounting for 90 percent of all forestry-related jobs. Though there are many smaller reservations on which forestry is a highly significant source of property income, the fourteen major tribes participating in forestry are by far the most important (Table 21).

Indian forests are managed by the BIA. The agency's functions encompass: (1) timber sale administration, including contract negotiation and enforcement, the marking and scaling of timber, and the collection and allotment of payments; (2) protecting the forests from pests and fires; (3) planning and surveying timber lands and setting standards for allowable cuts; and (4) developing forest resources through reforestation, afforestation, thinning, and pruning.

Table 21. Reservation Forest Operations, 1968

	COMMER- CIAL FOREST LAND (1,000 ACRES)	MBF° PRODUC- TION, 1968	STUMPAGE RECEIPTS (THOUSANDS)	QUALITY OF LUMBER (VALUE PER MBF°)	DIRECT INDIAN EMPLOY- MENT MAN- YEARS	DIRECT AND INDIRECT INDIAN EMPLOY- MENT MAN- YEARS
Total	5,349.0	951,813	$21,107,858	$22.18	2,369	3,320
Quinault	128.0	185,959	3,369	18.15	284	554
Colville	807.5	129,215	3,352	25.95	320	415
Yakima	482.2	132,181	3,281	24.82	80	208
Warm Springs	337.1	114,197	2,925	25.61	55	147
Hoopa Valley	81.2	68,941	2,880	41.78	167	224
Flathead	411.5	61,910	1,798	29.05	113	159
Fort Apache	719.7	73,574	935	12.71	394	454
Spokane	107.0	20,341	451	22.19	40	54
Navajo	464.8	36,928	371	10.04	465	526
Mescalero	187.6	21,228	305	14.38	14	25
Makah	25.2	11,049	260	23.57	31	57
Annette Island	21.2	5,345	172	32.17	20	26
Red Lake	336.7	13,694	130	9.51	86	100
San Carlos	117.5	9,813	100	10.16	42	49
All other	1,143.0	67,438	777	11.53	258	322

° Million board feet.

Source: Bureau of Indian Affairs.

The aim of these BIA functions is succinctly stated in its regulations: "The development of Indian forests by the Indian people for the purpose of promoting self-sustained communities, to the end that the Indians may receive from their own property not only stumpage value, but also the benefit of whatever profit it is capable of yielding and whatever labor the Indians are qualified to perform."[6] In other words, the BIA seeks to maximize the lease payments for the use of Indian forests, to develop reservation industries to utilize these resources, and to increase the employment opportunities for Indians.

The BIA has worked effectively to secure the highest possible cash income for Indians' forest resources. Because contracts for stumpage privileges are open to competitive bid and the BIA establishes minimum bids based on its own value estimates, a fair "market rate" is usually received. Even more important, the BIA has sought to increase the output and thus the stumpage receipts per acre through more intensive forest management procedures. With increased thinning and pruning, reforestation, fertilization, and more careful management generally, the sustained yield per acre can be markedly expanded. Without these activities, an increased yield cannot be sustained. Furthermore, the BIA will not permit the tribe to draw down its reserves. For instance, a 1967 study of the Flathead Indian reservation by the BIA found that its production could be increased from a 1965 output of 26,566 million board feet (MBF) and a 1966 output of 50,170 MBF to 60,000 MBF within the next few years and eventually to between 80,000 and 95,000 MBF, provided that management operations could be improved. The BIA subsequently expanded its activities, which permitted an increase in allowed and actual cut. Total management expenditures rose from $189,000 in 1966 to $307,-000 in 1968. Output could thereby be increased more than a fifth, with revenues rising by $1,974,000. Obviously, this more intensive management has been a profitable investment. On other reservations, specifically those with the largest forest areas, increased management outlays have resulted in substantially increased outputs and revenues.

The experience on reservations with less abundant or productive forests has been far less favorable. For many of these reservations, forest management outlays have equaled or exceeded the revenue from forest products. The revenue to outlay ratio for all but the largest seven producers is very close to one, and the investment of funds in many cases has not been warranted by the cash returns (Table 22). Noting the often unfavorable return on forestry expenditures, the

Table 22. Timber Outlays and Receipts, 1965–1968

YEAR	GROSS OUTLAY	GROSS CASH RECEIPTS	REVENUE/OUTLAY
Seven largest producing reservations			
1965	$1,765,601	$11,169,590	6.3
1966	1,832,064	12,948,229	7.1
1967	1,877,241	12,770,047	6.8
1968	2,017,616	13,561,506	6.7
All other reservations			
1965	$1,329,706	$1,124,148	.8
1966	1,361,396	1,344,461	1.0
1967	1,365,829	1,529,953	1.1
1968	1,729,286	1,838,494	1.1

Source: Bureau of Indian Affairs.

Bureau of the Budget has urged that management outlays be financed from a revolving fund providing loans for forestry purposes. Only "profitable" investments would then be undertaken, and the federal government would not be strapped with the management of marginal forests.

As the system now operates, a maximum of 10 percent of all stumpage revenues are charged as a management or administrative fee and returned to the federal Treasury. If the tribes spend money on their own, refunds are provided from the 10 percent fee in the same ratio as tribal funds relate to total costs. In some cases, such as on the Hoopa Valley, Navajo, Red Lake, and Yakima reservations, the tribes provide substantial portions of management funds. In most cases, however, tribal expenditures are small, amounting to only $394,000 in 1967, or a seventh of federal expenditures during that year.

Quite understandably, most tribes want the BIA to increase their forestry investments, since the tribes have to bear little, if any, of the cost and reap almost all the returns. This is sometimes a rather unproductive use of federal funds, and there are several presently managed Indian forests that are neither commercially profitable nor good investments in strict cost-benefit terms because management outlays may exceed cash revenues. Certainly, some of these operations should be curtailed and the funds transferred to other vital purposes.

But the ratio of commercial management expenditures to receipts should not be the sole controlling factor. There are many other benefits of forestry operations that cannot be measured by receipts and that are nevertheless of great importance. The employment effects are the most significant of these factors. The aggregate Indian wage bill was estimated at almost three-fourths of the total stumpage receipts in 1968. Though the stumpage receipts alone may not balance management outlays, the addition of the wages paid to Indians — wages which would otherwise not be received — may help justify the costs. Some management expenditures would be required even if there were no commercial use of the forest, and these expenses should be subtracted from the costs of commercial management. Also, it may be argued that earnings and payments from timber production are much more beneficial to the tribe and to the individual than an equal transfer payment. If these factors are considered, commercial forest management may be justified on many reservations where stumpage receipts fail to exceed outlays. As special consideration must be given to the needs of Indians, strict financial principles cannot always be rigidly applied.

Given its limited management budget, the BIA has done a good job of maximizing the sustained use of and cash income from reservation forests. Unfortunately, it has been far less effective in increasing Indian forestry employment and in promoting tribal and reservation-based forest-product industries.

Forestry is an important source of jobs on the major producing reservations. It is estimated that on the 13 (excluding the Navajo) reservations receiving the bulk of stumpage payments, direct employment in forestry amounted to 2,000

Indian man-years in 1968. This is substantial when compared with the 8,820 persons who were estimated to have been in the labor forces of these reservations; but nevertheless, Indians are filling only a small proportion of the jobs related to the use of their own resources. Indians accounted for less than a third of the 7,316 man-years of direct employment in forestry on all reservations in 1968. If the local jobs related to the use of forest products are considered, Indians held less than a fifth of the 9,510 additional man-years of employment in 1968.[7] These estimates are extremely crude but clearly indicate the meager share of Indian employment.

There are several ways in which this slim proportion could be increased. One would be for the tribes and the BIA to insist on Indian employment quotas from outside firms receiving stumpage privileges. An example of a tribe that employs this method is the Mescalero tribe, which requires that at least half the jobs in firms processing its timber be filled by its members. All tribal contracts have preferential hiring clauses or nondiscrimination provisions, but more jobs could be provided through employment quotas.

Such a measure would be pointless and self-defeating if there were no Indians who wanted or were qualified for jobs in forestry-related industries. In many cases Indians are not being hired only because they lack the requisite skills. Employment assistance has been used to help train Indians for better jobs, most notably on the Navajo reservation, and this has met with great success. Manpower training should certainly be expanded where needed, and subsidies should be given to private firms hiring and training Indians on the job.

But perhaps the best way to increase the Indian employment is to locate the timber processing firms on the reservation, preferably making them tribal enterprises. Tribally owned sawmills are now located on the Fort Apache, Jicarillo, Blackfeet, Red Lake, Warm Springs, and Navajo reservations, and independent Indian loggers operate mills on other reservations. Although these operations have had different degrees of success, they have definitely increased Indian employment. On the Navajo reservation, for example, almost all the direct employment positions are held by Indians. Its Navajo Forest Products Industries has demonstrated what tribally owned timber operations can achieve with good management. The Navajo reservation is not endowed with particularly good timber stands, yet the tribal corporation has been profitable and has provided a large Indian wage bill. In 1969, net profits were $1,574,000; Navajo wages and salaries were $1,803,000; and stumpage payments were $873,000. If the same enterprise had been located off the reservation, or if it had been owned by an outsider, only the stumpage and a small proportion of the wages would have been received by Indians.

Other tribally owned enterprises have not been so successful. The more modest success of operations on the Warm Springs reservation is more indicative of what will actually be accomplished. The Warm Springs operation earned profits of $427,000 in 1968 and paid Indian salaries of $345,000 and stumpage of $1,935,000. Since it probably has more potential than the Navajo operation because of its higher quality timber, the Warm Springs Indians have paid off its debt in a much shorter period of time. Some enterprises, such as the Red Lake sawmill which operated in the red until 1969, are bound to have difficulties; but most of the 14 largest producing reservations could internalize forestry operations through tribally owned enterprises, especially since they would not have to pay corporate taxes. Financial and organizational assistance will be needed from the BIA and other agencies, but the potential benefits seem well worth the time and expense. The profit and employment aspects of forestry operations should be stressed by the BIA and other manpower and industrial development agencies.

OIL, GAS, AND OTHER MINERALS

Of the many misconceptions about Indians, one of the least realistic and yet most persistent is the belief that a substantial number have grown, and continue to grow, rich from oil and gas. Unfortunately, such imagery often obscures reality. The facts are that few Indians now benefit from oil and gas revenues; these revenues presently make for very few millionaires; and few grew rich even in the past. Excluding the Osage tribe, Indians received an average annual total of nearly $7.0 million in oil and gas royalties since 1924.

Divided among several hundred thousand Indians, the royalties amount to very little per capita. Most of the "millionaires" created by oil and gas revenues were members of the small Osage tribe, which had 5,300 members in 1967. Blessed with highly productive oil lands, this single tribe received $368 million in royalties between 1924 and 1965. And during the 1920s, the average Osage Indian family received an annual income of $40,000 from the oil and gas receipts of the tribe. But oil prices have declined; the major reserves have been tapped; and the Osage population has grown. The 2,229 Osage "headrights," or inherited shares of tribal royalties, will return only $3,000 apiece in 1970 and half this amount on a per capita basis since there are two Osages for every headright.

Perhaps there will be other small groups of Indians to reap fortunes from as yet untapped oil reserves. Though most Alaskan land claims remain unsettled, the small Tyonek band of the Tlinget-Haida tribe, numbering 178 in 1968, has already established its claim to a reserve on Cook Inlet. In 1966 and 1967, it received $14 million in bonus bids and will undoubtedly receive more as oil is discovered.

However, these isolated cases of instant wealth do not help the hundreds of thousands of Indians who have little or no revenue from oil and gas. Though this is the single most important source of property income in the aggregate, it is also the most unequally distributed, with only a very small number of tribes receiving substantial amounts. In fiscal 1969, nine reservations received 85 percent of all royalties from oil and gas (Table 23). If the Navajo and Five Civilized Tribes are excluded, the remaining seven, with approximately 5 percent of the Indian reservation population, received more than half of all royalties.

The oil and gas resources on all Indian reservations except the Osage are "managed" by the BIA, which is largely limited to ensuring that legislative and administrative criteria are met in contracts with private firms for use of these resources. The exploration and development of Indian lands are left almost entirely in the hands of the private sector, and the only federal expenditures are for a few general geological surveys, which have no immediate payoff. There are no programs for exploring or developing potential oil and gas lands, no efforts to promote Indian employment in related industries, and no strategy to develop Indian-owned firms. As a result, vast areas of reservation lands lie unexplored and unused; Indian employment in the oil and gas industries on their own lands is inconsequential; and there are few Indian-owned drilling operations. The Osage tribe maintains its own management staff and has financed exploration

Table 23. Major Recipients of Oil and Gas Royalties, Fiscal
1969 (thousands)

Navajo	$8,566
Osage	7,013
Wind River	2,925
Five Civilized Tribes	1,802
Cononcity	1,696
Uintah-Ouray	1,590
Jicarillo Apache	1,428
Kiowa, Comanche, Apache, Oklahoma	1,159
Northern Cheyenne, Montana	1,098

Source: Bureau of Indian Affairs.

and mapping with an apparently high return, but other tribes spend no substantial amounts on their oil and gas resources. There is little doubt that a more active management policy would increase Indian oil and gas income, though it is impossible to predict the exact amount of increase. Certainly there is a need for immediate and accurate geological surveys.

As the system now works, however, private firms first conduct their own exploration, and then Indian oil and gas rights are opened for competitive bid. There are three types of payments involved in these bids. First, there is a minimum per acre rental, legislatively set at $1.25, which must be paid during the drilling stage until oil is discovered. Since large land tracts are required, there were more than 4 million acres of land rented for oil and gas use at the end of fiscal 1969. Obviously, the small per acre rentals mount up and are an important and constant source of income in the aggregate.

The major source of income, however, is the royalty payment, which is administratively fixed at no less than one-sixth of the return from whatever oil and gas is discovered. If lands have proven oil potential, the tribe may bargain for a higher royalty rate; but there are only a few exceptions where the royalty is set lower than the standard. In comparison, the rate for unproven federal and most private lands is one-eighth rather than one-sixth of the return. Reservations are, therefore, at a competitive disadvantage in attracting oil drillers, because most drillers will prefer lands where a lower royalty is demanded. Of course it is impossible to ascertain whether total income would be increased or decreased with a lower ratio, because the revenues are greater on reservations where oil is actually discovered than where royalties are one-eighth and oil is not discovered. If only to equalize the distribution of revenues, it might be better to use the lower rate to attract operations to those reservations with untapped potential.

The final source of revenue is the bonus, which is paid in a lump sum for lease rights. On unproven lands there may be little or no bonus, but on those with proven potential, bonuses can be substantial. For instance, the Tyonek band in Alaska was paid an $11.7 million bonus for the lease of 10,384 acres in 1966. Indians have often chosen higher bonus payments over increased royalties with a higher value during the life of the lease.

There is no way of knowing whether Indians have received the true value for their oil and gas resources and no reason to believe that they are in a less advantageous position than private landowners to bargain with private firms. But this does not deny the fact that greater investments in this area by the tribes and by the government could have as productive returns as they do in the management of forestry resources.

There are other valuable minerals on Indian lands, but they are of much less importance in the aggregate. In fiscal 1969, revenues from mineral rights other than oil and gas amounted to little over $4 million, or roughly an eighth of those from oil and gas. These other minerals are also unevenly distributed. The Laguna Pueblo reservation received $1,562,000 in fiscal 1969, mostly for uranium and vanadium, and the Navajo reservation received $778,000, mostly for the mining of uranium, vanadium, zinc, and coal. The Fort Hall reservation in Idaho received a royalty of $637,000, chiefly for the use of its phosphate reserves. Together, these three reservations received 71 percent of the royalties for minerals other than oil and gas in fiscal 1969.

As is the case with oil and gas reserves, the BIA concentrates its efforts on contract negotiation rather than resource development. Most surveys by the U.S. Geological Survey are conducted in response to specific proposals by private companies for the use of Indian minerals, and there is no general strategy to realize the mineral potential of reservation lands. There is a pressing need for a resources inventory to acquaint each tribe and the private sector with the reservation's mineral resources, and the Geological Survey, the BIA, and the tribes must make more active efforts to develop reservation resources to their maximum potential.

NOTES

1. BIA budget justification, fiscal 1970 (unpublished).

2. Bureau of Indian Affairs, "Land Use Inventory and Production Record," Report 50-1 for Calendar 1968. (Mimeographed.)

3. Stephen A. Langone, "The Heirship Land Problem and Its Effect on the Indian, the Tribe, and Effective Utilization," in *Toward Economic Development for Native American Communities*, Joint Economic Committee, 91st Cong., 1st Sess., 1969, vol. 2, p. 529.

4. William H. Veeder, "Federal Encroachment on Indian Water Rights and the Impairment of Reservation Development," in ibid., p. 469.

5. Cornell, Howlan, Hayes, and Merryfield, *A Study of the Indian Forest Program*, vol. 2, October 1968, p. 28.

6. U.S. Department of the Interior, Secretarial Regulations, "Objectives," 24 CFR 141.3 (1964).

7. Footnote 5.

"WE SHALL LEARN ALL THE DEVICES OF THE WHITE MAN.
WE SHALL HANDLE HIS TOOLS FOR OURSELVES.
WE SHALL MASTER HIS MACHINERY, HIS INVENTIONS,
        HIS SKILLS, HIS MEDICINE, HIS PLANNING;
BUT WE'LL RETAIN OUR BEAUTY
AND STILL BE INDIANS!"—DAVE MARTINNEZ, INSTITUTE OF AMERICAN INDIAN ARTS

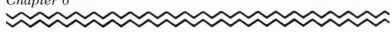

Chapter 6

Developing Economic and Human Resources

Even though reservations are endowed with valuable mineral resources and Indians receive substantial transfer payments from the government and from their tribes, the bulk of their income is earned through employment, much of it indeed related to natural resources. In the United States as a whole, about 70 percent of personal income is derived from wages and salaries, and the proportion of Indian income is very nearly the same. But because their earnings are meager, Indians usually live in poverty. They work intermittently, if at all, and typically their jobs are low-paying, unskilled, and unattractive. There is a critical and chronic job shortage in and around most reservations; at the same time Indians are usually ill-prepared for the few jobs which are available and are frequently discriminated against when they apply for jobs. The government accounts for a disproportionately large share of Indian employment, with private industrial and commercial enterprises providing jobs for less than 5 percent of the labor force on a man-year basis.

These severe employment problems can be measured in

Top: *Uintah and Ouray reservation. Glen Jenks, shown here working on a corral fence, is handy with a saw.* Bottom: *Indian school in Albuquerque, New Mexico, Sept. 1961. Vocational shop cabinet and mill; Mr. Robert Pacheco, teacher; special and regular program students.*

many ways. Perhaps most striking is the fact that less than one of every three Indians aged 16 or over is employed, compared with six of ten for the country as a whole. Because far fewer adults have jobs and much more of the Indian population is under 16, on the average only 18 persons out of each 100 on reservations work to support themselves and their dependents, while there are 38 for each 100 throughout the United States.

Unemployment is extremely high on the reservations, though technical problems make it difficult to apply the normal unemployment measures. The Bureau of the Census estimated that 17 percent of Indians aged 14 and over were unemployed in 1960. This considerably understated the problem, however, since only those who were actively seeking work were counted as unemployed if they did not hold jobs in the week preceding the census. Because jobs are scarce on or near reservations, many Indians are not seeking work even if they would welcome employment.

To secure more realistic estimates, the BIA began to compile its own employment statistics in 1963. Its measure of the labor force excludes only those who cannot work because of health problems, child care responsibilities, or school attendance; those who can work but are not seeking jobs are included among the unemployed. Using this definition, 42 percent of reservation Indians were unemployed in 1968, as indicated in Table 24. Such a high rate over-

Table 24. Distribution of Unemployment on 113 Reservations, 1968

PERCENT UNEMPLOYMENT	NUMBER OF RESERVATIONS	POPULATION
Total	113	356,495
Under 10	10	3,762
10–29	25	44,490
30–49	43	96,738
50–69	29	192,318
70 and over	6	19,188

Source: Computed from BIA, *Summary of Reservation Development Studies and Analyses,* August, 1969.

states the problem if it is used as a comparison with national rates, which averaged 3.6 percent in 1968 according to the Census Bureau definition. National unemployment, if the BIA measure were used, would be severalfold higher than the reported rate. Even so, unemployment on Indian reservations would be at least three times the national rate, and there is little doubt that it is critically high.

There are also high levels of underemployment and seasonal employment. In a study prepared for the Joint Economic Committee of the United States Congress, Alan Sorkin found that peak unemployment during the winter months is 70 percent higher than during the summer months when jobs are more plentiful because of agricultural work.[1] In a survey of five Indian reservations, Taylor and O'Connor found that the proportion of Indians aged 16 and over who worked for more than 10 months during the year ranged from a low of 12 percent on one reservation to a high of 36 percent on another reservation.[2] The nature of farming and related rural occupations, with a variety of chores, does not generally afford much opportunity for complete idleness even on small or marginal farming units. For example, while the Navajo sheepherder is not completely unemployed, neither can it be claimed that he is gainfully employed or that the income from his occupation is sufficient to support himself and his family. The problem on Indian reservations is therefore not only one of unemployment but also of underemployment.

Working Indians are also concentrated at the lower end of the employment totem, in part reflecting their rural residence. Over half of the male Indians employed in 1960 were farmers and laborers compared with one-sixth of employed males nationally. Only 1 of every 10 working Indian women had clerical or related jobs compared with 3 in 10 nationally. Few rural Indians held skilled positions, since only about 4 percent of all males and 9 percent of females were professional, technical, and kindred workers compared with 11 and 13 percent nationally. Similarly, there were few in entrepreneurial and managerial jobs, with less than 2 percent of the male and female Indians being nonfarm managers, officials, and proprietors; the national rates were 11 percent for males and 4 percent for females.

An inordinate proportion of full-time jobs held by Indians is with the federal government. Big Brother is the most important employer on reservations. The BIA employed an estimated 8,345 Indians full time as of November 30, 1969, the IHS an additional 3,200, while OEO, EDA, and other federal agencies employed hundreds more. This accounts for a huge share of total nonagricultural employment. It was estimated, for instance, that industrial and commercial enterprises located on or near reservations provided only 6,000 man-years of employment in fiscal 1969, compared with the 11,500 in the IHS and BIA alone.

Unfortunately, Indians are concentrated in low-level jobs even when the government is their employer. The following table showing the distribution of wage and salary workers in BIA and IHS indicates that Indians are concentrated in the lower pay scales. Though Indians fill more than half of the jobs within BIA, they hold less than a fifth of the top executive jobs which pay more than $14,000. Likewise, in the Indian Health Service only 18 percent of the Indians who are employed are paid more than $8,000 compared with two-thirds of all other workers.

According to all these measures, the employment problems of Indians on reservations are severe. Though they cannot be attacked apart from the other Indian problems, there are two basic approaches which must be taken. Efforts are obviously needed to increase the number of jobs which are available to Indians on or near reservations. More private firms must be attracted to the environs, while tribes and individuals should be increasingly assisted in initiating their own industrial and commercial enterprises. At the

Table 25. Distribution of BIA and IHS Wage and Salaried Employees, Fiscal 1970

ANNUAL EARNINGS LEVEL	WAGE WORKERS				SALARIED EMPLOYEES			
	BIA		IHS		BIA		IHS	
	TOTAL OF EMPLOYEES IN CATEGORY	INDIANS AS PERCENTAGE OF TOTAL IN CATEGORY	TOTAL OF EMPLOYEES IN CATEGORY	INDIANS AS PERCENTAGE OF TOTAL IN CATEGORY	TOTAL OF EMPLOYEES IN CATEGORY	INDIANS AS PERCENTAGE OF TOTAL IN CATEGORY	TOTAL OF EMPLOYEES IN CATEGORY	INDIANS AS PERCENTAGE OF TOTAL IN CATEGORY
Total	3,298	77	1,154	85	12,225	47	4,342	51
Under $5,000	76	89	192	95	188	96	309	96
$ 5,000–$ 6,499	929	91	373	93	3,651	86	1,567	79
$ 6,500–$ 7,999	1,174	82	255	91	1,743	60	698	46
$ 8,000–$ 9,999	778	61	248	72	3,804	24	1,209	25
$10,000–$13,999	271	55	83	35	1,260	22	261	16
$14,000–$17,999	65	63	2	50	1,221	16	219	7
$18,000 and over	5	—	1	—	358	17	79	16

Source: Bureau of Indian Affairs and Indian Health Service.

same time, efforts must also be expanded to improve the productivity of the Indian work force through manpower training, and to provide whatever other labor market services may be needed to put Indians to work. Manpower and economic development programs must work hand in hand to strengthen the economies and human resources of the reservations.

INDUSTRIAL AND COMMERCIAL DEVELOPMENT

OBSTACLES TO ECONOMIC DEVELOPMENT

There are some very good reasons why more businesses are not located on reservations, or near enough to hire a substantial number of Indians.[3] Most reservations are inaccessible to product markets because of their geographical isolation and the lack of adequate transportation facilities. With their low average income and typically widespread settlement, reservation Indians provide only a limited market themselves for any products. The Indian labor force is generally unskilled; and because of their poor education, Indians may be expensive to train. Though many may be unemployed on a reservation, only a limited number are available for work at a single point because of the dispersion of population. With differing cultural attitudes, Indians find it difficult to adapt to sustained employment and job discipline, and the result is higher labor cost due to absenteeism and seasonal turnover, at least in the early stages of operation.

There is also a shortage of capital for public and private investment. Financial institutions are unfamiliar with reservations and are unwilling to take the high risks often involved in lending to Indians, especially since lands, which are the Indians' major asset, cannot be taken as collateral on loans. Public funds are equally limited, and the few tribes with substantial resources are reluctant to use them for commercial and industrial purposes.

Besides their poor transportation systems, reservations generally lack the other social overhead capital, such as sewerage and electrical facilities, needed to attract businesses. Competing with many other localities for the limited number of new and relocating firms, reservations are usually at a disadvantage because they cannot offer the amenities available elsewhere.

To complicate matters, there is little knowledge about conditions on reservations. Businessmen do not know what to expect since there is usually little information available on labor forces, prevailing wage rates, skill levels, worker attitudes, and overhead capital. All these factors can vitally affect the profitability of any operation. There is an equally severe shortage of trained personnel on the reservations to coordinate industrial development efforts; tribal leaders, who are often elderly, are sometimes unqualified for or disinterested in planning and administering such programs. Faced with these uncertainties, businessmen understandably turn their attention to more predictable locations for their investments.

ECONOMIC DEVELOPMENT PROGRAMS

A number of federal programs aim at alleviating these problems and promoting the industrial and commercial development of the reservations. Several agencies are involved. For instance, the Small Business Administration (SBA) has extended its loan programs to Indians. In fiscal 1968, 45 business loans were made to Indian entrepreneurs, averaging nearly $30,000, and this total was increased slightly in fiscal 1969.[4] The Office of Economic Opportunity finances various efforts to train tribal leaders in business management, also funding a staff of economic development specialists to provide assistance to those reservations which are not served by other programs. The Department of Housing and Urban Development approved $3.4 million in neighborhood facilities grants during fiscal 1967–1969 to finance improvements which would increase the attractiveness and possibly the profitability of reservation business locations. But the most significant programs, and the ones most directly concerned with industrial and commercial development, are those of the EDA and the BIA.

There are 107 reservations, containing four-fifths of all reservation Indians, which are designated as economic development areas and are eligible to receive EDA assistance.[5] The EDA has a separate desk for Indian affairs and is placing increasing emphasis on the development of reservations by allocating nearly 10 percent of its resources for Indian projects.

The EDA provides three types of assistance: (1) technical assistance and planning grants; (2) financing for public works projects; and (3) loans to businesses locating in or near target areas. In helping reservations, EDA places more than the normal stress on the first two types of assistance. Because of the backward state of reservation economies, it is assumed that social overhead capital, planning, and technical assistance are needed before businesses can be developed or attracted on a large scale.

Public works, in particular, have accounted for the bulk of EDA commitments (Table 26). Financing for these projects usually amounts to the maximum 80 percent grant plus a low-interest-rate, long-term loan for the remaining 20 percent. Beginning in late 1970, EDA had authority to

Table 26. EDA Approvals, 1966–1970
(amounts in thousands)

	FIVE-YEAR TOTAL	PERCENT OF TOTAL	1966	1967	1968	1969	1970
Total	$77,831	100	$3,240	$22,472	$18,688	$17,428	$16,003
Public works	56,718	73	1,353	15,978	14,443	15,238	9,706
Business loans	17,762	23	1,773	6,018	3,478	584	5,909
Technical assistance and planning	3,351	4	114	476	767	1,606	388

Source: U.S. Department of Commerce, Economic Development Administration.

make 100 percent grants for public works. These public works expenditures are allocated for a variety of purposes, with major emphasis on industrial parks and tourist and reservation projects. There were 25 of each type of project as of March 31, 1970, and these accounted for 57 percent of the public works approvals on reservations, with $6.7 million going for the former and $24 million for the latter.

Industrial parks concentrate expenditures in a single area of a reservation. Because of the dearth of overhead capital, this is often the only way that limited funds can have any impact in attracting firms. It is hoped that a growth node can be created which will be the focus of sustained expansion. Because Indian populations are often scattered, the creation of a large number of jobs in a single locality can overload its housing, educational, and other community facilities as Indians move in, searching for employment. There is also the problem of the choice of location and, in some cases, the immediate payoff in terms of attracting businesses and collecting rentals has been given a higher priority than the long-term growth effects. The industrial parks on some reservations, such as the Gila River in Arizona, are located on the periphery, close to urban complexes, but far from the center of Indian population.

Tourism facilities usually involve considerable expenditures, but the return can also be large and immediate, with increased income flowing into the area and heavy spillover effects on employment and tourist-related businesses. Though there are 25 approved tourism projects, a handful account for the bulk of EDA public works approvals. For instance, the projects on the nine reservations listed in Table 27 accounted for $16 million, or two-thirds of all tourist approvals. Twelve other reservations received the remainder, making a total of 21 with EDA-supported tourism projects.

Technical assistance and planning grants have been given

Table 27. EDA Recreation and Tourism Project Approvals, 1967–1970

RESERVATION	FISCAL YEAR APPROVAL	EDA FUNDS (MILLIONS)
Navajo	1967	$2.0
Warm Springs	1967	3.1
Warm Springs	1968	1.2
Uintah-Ouray	1967	1.4
Fort Apache	1968	1.6
Menominee	1968	1.0
Fort Berthold	1969	1.1
San Carlos	1969	1.2
Standing Rock	1970	1.2
Mescalero	1970	2.3

Source: Economic Development Administration.

to a large number of reservations. These cover up to 75 percent of the costs, with the remainder contributed by the tribe or by other agencies, often the OEO. The technical assistance grants are mostly used to study the feasibility of specific proposals, while planning grants finance a professional staff of economic developers serving Indian reservations. There can be little doubt that planning, technical assistance, and tribal participation in development are necessary foundations for economic development. Unfortunately, some of the money for these purposes has not been spent productively. For instance, the Overall Economic Development Plans prepared under EDA planning grants vary widely in quality, but most have little useful information and are now laid to rest in the files of the Commerce Department. Technical assistance has been linked directly with public works projects to test their feasibility and probable effect. Little has been learned which is of use for anything outside of these projects. Clearly, more is needed in the way of general information to attract businesses to reservations, and this information must be made readily available.

Business loan activity has been limited, with only 25 loans through March 31, 1970, but it is anticipated that the number will increase rapidly as the industrial parks are completed and firms find it feasible to locate on reservations. This is, in fact, already occurring; business loans rose from $3.5 million in fiscal 1968 and—despite a drop to $0.6 million in fiscal 1969—to $5.9 million in the first nine months of fiscal 1970. These loans carry a low interest rate, cover up to 65 percent of the investment costs, and are made either to the tribe or directly to the business, depending upon whether the tribe wants to assume responsibility for the debt. Table 28 lists the seven reservations which were the major recipients, accounting for 64 percent of approved loan funds.

The major shortcoming of EDA's efforts, one which is characteristic of those outside the reservations as well, is that its resources have been demanded and received by areas of lesser growth potential. Originally, EDA's intent was to concentrate expenditures on the 15 reservations which seemed to have the best prospects; these contained about half of all reservation Indians. But 107 reservations are presently designated as economic development areas, and from July 1967 through November 1968 reservations other than the primary 15 received 56 percent of the total allocated funds; or in other words, areas with less growth potential received more funds on a per capita basis.

Table 28. EDA Business Loans by Type and Reservation

RESERVATION	BUSINESS	AMOUNT APPROVED (THOUSANDS)
Fort Apache	Lumber processing	$4,387
Cattanaugus, N.Y.	Lumber processing	1,960
Papago	Harlan metals	1,203
Yakima	Lumber processing	1,001
Santo Domingo	Lumber processing	978
Gila River	Del Ray feeding	801

Source: Economic Development Administration.

BIA ECONOMIC DEVELOPMENT

The BIA is also involved in economic development on a large scale, with programs focusing on four areas: (1) transportation, (2) credit and finance, (3) technical assistance, and (4) locational subsidies. In fiscal 1970, the BIA spent nearly $25 million on the construction and maintenance of Indian roads, though only a small proportion of these have a direct impact on economic development by serving existing or projected business enterprises. Credit and financing provided by the BIA amounted to around $2 million, but only a small proportion went for economic development purposes. Technical assistance, training, and planning expenditures constituted an additional $6.6 million, and employment assistance provided training subsidies of another $2 million, which may have helped to attract new firms to the reservation. Because the data are skimpy, attempts to qualify the exact expenditures by the BIA on economic development are illusive; they are less than those of the EDA, but still important.

A serious impediment to the economic development of Indian reservations is their generally inadequate transportation system. On the 55 million acres of reservation and allotted land, there were only 9,500 miles of paved roads in mid-1970, and over 4,000 miles of gravel roads. Even counting those which are unsurfaced and may be impassable much of the year, there was a total of only 44,032 miles in 1969 (Table 29).

Quantitatively and qualitatively, this road system is far below the standards of surrounding areas. For instance, the Navajo-Hopi reservation has only 56 miles of all-weather road mileage per 1,000 square miles of area, compared with 150 miles per 1,000 square miles in Arizona, New Mexico, and Utah. The Pine Ridge, Zuñi, Crow, Papago, and Colville reservations have on the average only 36 percent of the all-weather roads per unit area as their surround-

Table 29. Road mileage by type, 1969

	TOTAL	PAVED	GRAVEL	UNSURFACED
Total	44,032	8,751	4,035	31,246
State highways	5,983	5,300	400	283
County	16,034	1,605	1,729	12,700
BIA	18,492	1,695	1,856	14,941
Tribal	1,935	6	18	1,911
Other	1,588	145	32	1,411

Source: Bureau of Indian Affairs.

ing states. To make matters worse, the limited mileage of existing roads is poorly maintained. The BIA allocated $4.3 million in fiscal 1970 or $358 per mile for regular road maintenance, compared with an estimated $635 per mile spent by state and local governments for blacktop roads. In fiscal 1970, 770 miles were added to the Indian system, with the BIA allocating an estimated $20 million and providing more than half the funds for this construction.

Public expenditures on highways and access roads can provide the impetus for growth, and there is little doubt that improvement in the transportation systems of reservations is one of their primary needs. From the economic development perspective, state highways may be the most important; but improved internal transportation is also a necessity, especially in bringing the dispersed populations to focal points of employment and commerce. For instance, the industrial parks built under the EDA program, almost all of which are located on existing highways, must be linked to the more remote parts of the reservations if Indians are to benefit to the fullest degree.

Another BIA program aiming at the economic development of reservations is its credit and financing operation, providing loans for business as well as other purposes. Unfortunately, the scale of the program is almost totally inadequate to the need. In 1969 the BIA's revolving loan fund,

established under several different legislative acts, had
$25.3 million in outstanding loans, but only $1.8 million
was loaned in that year, and $2.6 million in the preceding
fiscal year. Indians presently get credit from other sources —
private institutions, other government programs, and tribal
funds — which dwarf BIA's efforts. An estimated $145.7
million in loans were made in 1968 by customary lenders,
including other government credit agencies, with outstand-
ing loans of tribal funds increasing by $12.8 million between
1968 and 1969. But almost all of this was consumer credit,
and the amounts going for business purposes, outside of
SBA and EDA loans, are minuscule. While the BIA estimates
that Indians need in excess of $230 million to finance com-
mercial and industrial development, probably less than
$20 million goes for this purpose annually.[6]

Several bills have been introduced which would open up
new sources of credit for economic development, but none
of these has as yet been accepted. The most comprehensive
is the Indian Financing Act of 1970, which would expand
direct loan funds, provide for loan guarantees and insurance
of private loans, and authorize payment of interest subsidies
and administrative expenses. Indians oppose the provision
that lands purchased with the loan funds could be put up as
security for loans. This would increase the flow of private
funds to reservations, since Indians often have no other
collateral of value, but there would also be a chance that
some Indian lands purchased with the funds would be eroded
by defaults on loans. In 1969, 18.5 percent of the repayments
due on loans from the revolving fund were either delinquent
or in default, and this high loss rate raises questions of whether a strict loan program would ever be feasible.[7]

Even if credit could be expanded, it is not at all clear that
Indians would borrow on a large scale for business purposes.
Indian trust funds now contain more than $300 million; over
the years tribes have invested only $46.5 million of this

amount for commercial and industrial development. Some tribes do not invest in their own economic development because they feel it is too risky. Also, many of the needed investments, especially those on social overhead capital, produce no immediate revenue from which debts can be repaid. Certainly credit should be made available for those tribes which can and will use it productively for economic development, but the Financing Act would not be a panacea for Indian economic woes.

The third BIA economic development effort is the provision of technical assistance and planning funds to Indian tribes. This comes from three principal sources: (1) Under its credit operations, the BIA allocated nearly $2 million in fiscal 1970 to provide technical assistance to Indian organizations for the management and operation of credit programs and tribal enterprises. (2) An additional $2.3 million was allocated for basic information gathering on demography, natural resources, and program operations, and the data generated in this process may be useful in attracting business firms. (3) Finally, $1.3 million in fiscal 1970 was provided for cooperative activity, economic feasibility studies, and management training. Thus a total of some $6.6 million was expended on training, technical assistance, and planning for economic development by the BIA.

The final BIA program concerned with economic development provides on-the-job training (OJT) subsidies of up to half of the minimum wage over a negotiated training period. The private employer contracting for these subsidies agrees to fill a stipulated number of OJT slots with Indians. As of January 1, 1970, there were 184 businesses which had contracted for these subsidies, and they employed 5,960 Indians, paying $1.85 per hour on the average. Subsidies averaged over $1,000 per trainee, compared with the $3,000 average annual training subsidy under the JOBS program.

Though the subsidy is not large, and many of the contract-

ing businesses were already in existence, and though a few
of those moving onto the reservation and receiving subsidies
might have moved there anyway, the BIA's program must
be credited with some effect in increasing the number of
jobs on the reservation. But its effectiveness alone has perhaps not been as great as when it has been used along with
other types of assistance. For instance, four-fifths of the
firms receiving EDA business loans to locate on the reservations also received BIA training subsidies.

ECONOMIC DEVELOPMENT POLICY

It is difficult to assess the aggregate impact of these industrial
and commercial development efforts. The EDA estimates
that 3,000 Indian jobs have been created by its efforts over
the past half-decade, and the BIA claims 6,000 remain as a
result of its own efforts since the early 1950s. But there is
almost complete overlap between the two. The decline in
unemployment rates as computed by the BIA—from 48 percent in 1965 to 40 percent in 1970—appears to be evidence
of these programs and perhaps of the tightening of labor
markets nationally during the 1960s.

Lacking better aggregate statistics, the temptation is to
turn to case studies, but this can be misleading. The most
publicized example of industrial development is the Fairchild semiconductor plant on the Navajo reservation at Shiprock, New Mexico. It employs some 1,200 Indians, or one-
fifth of those claimed to be employed as a result of BIA
expenditures for industrial development. The plant will
receive almost half of the BIA's OJT funds in fiscal 1970,
and it has also received two EDA business loans totalling
$678,000. The Navajo tribe initially contributed the use
of one of its community buildings, and all these factors have
figured in the success of the operation. But the case is atyp-
ical to the extreme, since 160 of the 184 industrial and com-

mercial enterprises which BIA has assisted have fewer than 100 Indian employees, and 59 have fewer than 10. Not only is the Shiprock plant in a class by itself, but it is unlikely that its experience can be replicated elsewhere. The Navajo reservation accounts for nearly 30 percent of total potential reservation labor supply. It is doubtful whether any other reservation could supply the labor force needed for a plant of the Shiprock size.

Whatever the accomplishments to date, the continuing economic plight of most reservations makes it clear that much remains to be done. While there are many programs focusing on the separate ingredients of industrial and commercial development, there is no agency with authority over the whole process. As a result, there has been no comprehensive statement of economic development policy. Questions remain unanswered about what is needed, both quantitatively and qualitatively, or for that matter the extent and type of economic development favored by Indians.

The quantitative goals in the economic development of reservations are sometimes distorted by the relative seriousness of the problems; there is a high rate of unemployment on reservations, and there are very few private sector jobs relative to the size of the labor force, but the absolute shortfalls are large and the rate of unemployment is critical on all large reservations. It would take some 60,000 jobs to bring the level of employment on reservations near the national level, and improved economic opportunities might attract many Indians back to the reservations. Still the task of industrial development is not insurmountable in a growing and expanding national economy. It can be crudely projected that most of the problems could be solved with another plant of the Shiprock size, around 10 hiring 500 Indians, 20 with 250, 40 of around 100, and maybe 100 of smaller size. This is a large number of plants, but it is not inconceivable that a good number of them could be attracted within a decade with proper incentives, and if labor markets tighten nationally. Of course not all the added employment would have to come from the new industrial and commercial enterprises.

It is also important to make the qualitative goals of economic development more explicit. Up to the present, with the dearth of jobs on the reservations, BIA could not be very selective in assisting firms to locate there. The main attraction was the low wages which could be paid because of the labor reserves, and the obvious result is that low-wage employment has been attracted. The average hourly wage rate for the 5,491 jobs generated by BIA through fiscal 1969 was only $1.82, or only $3,700 annually, for those who secured gainful employment year-round. While this is better than nothing, it certainly does not provide an adequate income for the large Indian families. The quality of jobs will have to be considered along with the quantity in designing incentives for firms to locate on reservations.

One especially critical qualitative aspect is that most of the jobs being created employ women rather than men. Alan Sorkin found that for nine manufacturing firms he visited, with a total of 1,370 employees, 71 percent of trainees were women. At the Fairchild semiconductor plant at Shiprock, this is an especially serious problem, with more than four of every five employees being women. This has had deleterious effects on family life in many cases, since the men cannot find equal employment opportunities. In recognition of this problem, a machine operation is being started at Shiprock which will employ only men, but this will not come close to creating a balance.

It is obvious that if a large number of substantial firms are to be attracted to or developed on reservations—firms which pay more than minimal wages and hire males in a larger proportion—significantly greater incentives must be offered. Expenditures on the social overhead capital of reservations must be expanded, and the tribes must be provided with the necessary financing for their development. But at the same time, some increased inducements must be given to non-Indian firms to attract them to the reservations. The 80 cents per hour maximum BIA subsidy for a limited term is not enough, nor is the low interest rate of the EDA's business loan.

The use of tax incentives to induce firms to locate on reservations offers an alternative. Tax credits could be given based on the number of Indians hired, thus encouraging Indian employment; and accelerated depreciation allowances could be offered to promote investment and to help attract more capital intensive industries. This approach, however, is fraught with difficulties. For instance, unless differential tax subsidies are given for different reservations, firms would move to the more attractive areas, not benefiting the poorer reservations. But differential schedules are so complex and difficult to administer that this alone could undermine the plan.

Increased direct locational subsidies might be preferable to tax incentives. This would require intensifying the present BIA training subsidies and would remove the fiction that they are actually tied to real differential training outlays. Indian economic development could in fact be accomplished without any new tools, if increased funding were provided for EDA's programs, if the other agencies stepped up their efforts, and if the BIA were permitted to increase its direct subsidy and were provided the funds to do so. Perhaps only in this way can the reservations become independent and viable economic areas.

FEDERAL MANPOWER PROGRAMS

Unless more jobs are provided on or near the reservations, Indians will continue to have low employment rates; but there are many existing jobs which Indians could hold if they were qualified. Without improvements in the labor force, it is unlikely that industrial and commercial development can proceed, so that manpower programs must be coordinated with economic development efforts.

There are many cultural factors which can impair Indian labor force participation. A major obstacle is that Indians often speak English poorly, having a limited command of the language and especially of the industrial lexicon. Another obstacle is that few Indians are time-oriented, in the sense that they plan their activities by the clock. This makes it difficult to adjust to factory discipline. Many Indians do not carefully plan for the future. For instance, they will abandon full-time, year-round jobs for attractive summer employment even though this means losing their stable employment. Usually Indians value landholdings and open spaces, and they prefer to live in isolated units rather than in congested areas. As a result, they are often scattered around the countryside and, with the poor transportation system, are unable to get to a place of work.

Such cultural factors are significant and can add to the costs of hiring Indians, as well as to their difficulty in finding and holding jobs. Yet, these obstacles are relatively easy to overcome. At the Fairchild semiconductor plant in Shiprock, New Mexico, for instance, instructions, procedures, and expectations have been adjusted fairly successfully to these cultural differences. Industrial terms have been added to the Indian language or approximate translations used; "aluminum" was converted to the Navajo phrase for "shiny metal," and "oscillator" became "tunnel."[8] Time schedules were adjusted, with the clocks in the plant being divided into ten sections, painted red and white alternatively and numbered consecutively. Thus, a six-minute "section" was used as the basic unit of time rather than minutes and hours. Problems in attracting workers to the area and retaining them at their jobs were solved by offering adequate wages and opportunities for upgrading. The lesson has been that where jobs are dependable, higher paying, and with avenues upward, many Indians are willing to modify their own life styles. Thus, cultural factors should not be exaggerated as obstacles to productive employment.

What Indians lack is much more basic and much more difficult to overcome—they generally lack the skills and the knowledge to be productive workers. The educational attainment of Indians, as noted earlier, is substantially below national norms, and the education they receive is often inferior. Because they have not had job opportunities in the past, and because outside training opportunities are limited, they have acquired few skills. As education improves, so will the abilities of the labor force, but more direct steps need to be taken through remedial training and basic education, along with the other manpower services which Indians may require to find employment and to improve their productivity and earnings. One such effort by the BIA is a literacy program for 75,000 functionally illiterate adults.

BIA MANPOWER PROGRAMS

The BIA has provided its own manpower services to Indians on reservations for almost two decades. Until recently, these were almost the only efforts made on behalf of Indians, and they still are of great significance, despite the extension of Labor Department programs to the reservations. Nearly 9,600 entered BIA's employment assistance or manpower programs in fiscal 1970, and they received services costing more than $33 million, or over $3,000 per person. Though BIA's efforts may be less extensive than those of the Labor Department, they are significantly more intensive (Table 30).

These programs are grouped administratively into two categories: Direct Employment and Adult Vocational Train-

Table 30. BIA Employment Assistance Programs, Fiscal Year 1970

PROGRAM	TOTAL EXPENDITURE (THOUSANDS)	ARRIVALS FOR D.E. AND ENTRIES INTO TRAINING	TOTAL SERVED
Total	$33,346	9,584	13,432
Direct Employment	11,797	3,757	4,213
Urban placement	*	853	853
Placement on or near reservation	*	2,000	2,000
Training centers	*	904	1,360
Adult Vocational Training	21,549	5,827	9,219
On-the-job	2,385	1,892	3,715
Institutional	19,164	3,935	5,504

° Not available.
Source: Bureau of Indian Affairs.

ing programs. Under the first, Indians can be placed on jobs on or near the reservations, or may be helped in finding urban jobs. Assistance is provided in the form of moving allowances, temporary subsidies, medical services, placement, and counseling. Also using Direct Employment program funds, three "experimental" residential training centers are operated, providing basic education and vocational training to entire Indian families who are so seriously disadvantaged that they cannot benefit from other training opportunities. On the other hand, the Adult Vocational Training program accounts for the bulk of training. Institutional courses are offered both near reservations and at vocational centers in larger urban areas which serve a number of reservations. The services and training under the institutional program are directed at individuals rather than families and differ in emphasis from that given in the three residential centers. On-the-job training is also funded under Adult Vocational Training, and this can provide placement, counseling, health, and other services for participants, though usually it funds only wage subsidies to employers, covering up to one-half of the minimum hourly wage for some training period. This subsidy has been used to attract employers to reservations and to induce them to hire Indians, so that it was also mentioned in the context of BIA's industrial and commercial development programs. Expenditures and participants under these various manpower efforts are broken down in Table 30.

Under the Direct Employment, the BIA attempts to assist each applicant who applies, Indian origin and residence "on or near" a reservation being the only criteria for eligibility. Although there is no training component, some individuals who have received assistance may have participated in Adult Vocational Training. Direct Employment is designed to assist those individuals who have a salable vocational skill for which there is no outlet in the Indian community. Based on individual needs, a wide variety of services—including interviewing, testing, counseling, and health care —are available. Perhaps most important are subsistence grants until placement. On the average, a single individual can get up to $184 per month if he is a commuter to a job on or near the reservation, or $315 if he is placed in an urban area. For a couple with three children, the rates rise to $358 and $820, respectively. An individual interested in being placed within commuting distance may be at his new job within two weeks, while relocation may take two months or perhaps more if the individual has some significant problem. Placement at the destination, however, is rapid. More than 40 percent of the relocatees are placed within one week and nearly 30 percent more by the end of the second week. Total costs for individuals provided Direct Employment services in fiscal 1970 averaged $2,785 per person.

The critical issue underlying the Direct Employment program is whether assistance should be used to relocate Indians to urban areas where jobs are more readily available or to help them find jobs on or near the reservations. Fluctuations in the funding levels reflect a shift in national policy concerning the most appropriate method of serving reservation Indians. Direct Employment—and termination—were obvious tactics of the dominant philosophy of the early 1950s, which favored integrating Indians into the economic mainstream. Disappointment with the effectiveness of such efforts, opposition from Indian groups rueing the loss of their best human resources, increasing job opportunities resulting from industrial and commercial development, and greater awareness of the plight of urban Indians led to a change in emphasis. And, as noted above, current policy aims to make the reservations themselves viable economic units. Hence, there is far more accent on locating jobs on or near reservations (Table 31).

Almost all studies of the relocation effort have agreed that Indians working in urban areas earn substantially more than those placed on or near reservations, but that very few successfully adapt to urban life. For instance, a 1968 BIA follow-up of 1963 placements in urban areas found that almost three-fourths had moved back to or near the reservation. Careful but dated records of the BIA from 1953 to 1957 found that five out of ten Indians returned within the first year. Others have estimated that between one-half and two-thirds of all relocatees eventually return to the reservation.[9]

Whatever success relocation may have in raising wage rates and income, the costs are not justified if clients return

Table 31. Direct Employment Placements, Selected Years, 1952–1970

FISCAL YEAR	TOTAL	EMPLOYMENT TRAINING CENTERS	PERCENT	ON OR NEAR RESERVATIONS	PERCENT	URBAN AREAS	PERCENT
1952	442	*	*	*	*	442	100.0
1958	2,373	*	*	63	2.7	2,310	97.3
1964	1,985	*	*	254	12.8	1,731	87.2
1968	2,928	718	24.5	1,136	38.8	1,074	36.7
1969	2,975	612	20.6	1,614	54.2	749	25.2
1970	3,757	904	24.1	2,000	53.2	853	22.7

* Component not yet in operation.
Source: Bureau of Indian Affairs.

without gaining skills or saving money. On the other hand, those who want to leave the reservation should be helped, since urban areas still offer greater opportunities. The BIA has therefore reversed its earlier preference for relocation and is trying to walk the tightrope of assisting without advocating relocation.

Intensive services costing around $5,000 per trainee are provided in the three residential centers funded under the Direct Employment program, operating in Roswell, New Mexico; Madera, California; and Fort Lincoln, North Dakota. To be eligible, a single individual or family head must lack a skill, have the equivalent of fewer than nine years of education, and be unqualified for institutional training. These centers take care of the whole family of the participant, offering adults a wide range of assistance, including intensive and innovative basic education, skill training, and home economics instruction, as well as job placement. Day care is provided for younger children. Between the beginning of the program in 1967 and June 1969, 1,600 persons had entered the centers, with 700 completers, and only 450 dropouts, a relatively low rate for this type of effort. Most of those concerned with the program are enthusiastic, but there is no way yet to measure effectiveness.

Institutional training is provided on a much larger scale under Adult Vocational Training and is intended primarily for those 18 to 35 years of age. In fiscal 1969, 2,700 persons entered training, two-thirds of whom attended institutions in Chicago, Cleveland, Dallas, Denver, Los Angeles, Oakland, or San Jose, while the remaining third received training on or near the reservation. Enrollees in the program receive the same types of health and counseling services and grants as those in the Direct Employment program, plus subsistence payments throughout the training period. In addition, however, they receive tuition and related costs for vocational training, so that costs run over $5,000 per enrollee. Institutional courses typically last about 10 months, but some trainees remain in school for two years. Some 1,800 courses in nearly 600 public and private schools have been accredited by BIA.

The BIA's institutional training program has demonstrated its effectiveness in increasing the employability and earnings of participants. The five-year follow-up of 1963 enrollees found that their earnings had increased severalfold over preenrollment levels. Those who went to urban training centers and then found jobs in these areas received much higher wages, but as under the Direct Employment program, many gradually drifted back to the reservation over time. Here again, the question arises whether it is a wise strategy to transport reservation Indians to urban training centers where they will be prepared for existing jobs within the area. The answer again is uncertain, but there is little evidence that those who receive training are any more likely to remain in the cities than those who are simply relocated. Accordingly, training opportunities are being increased near the reservation, and the portion of participants who are sent off to urban institutes is being reduced. In fiscal 1970, over 60 percent received institutional training near reservations.

In a minor component of the institutional program, about 40 families, primarily headed by widowed or unmarried women with children, are enrolled in the Solo Parent program in San Diego, California. In providing a residential setting, child care services, and home economics training, this program is similar to the education and training centers. However, enrollees in the Solo Parent program receive instruction at accredited public or private schools, rather than basic education and training.

The OJT segment of Adult Vocational Training is becoming increasingly important as industrial and commercial development efforts progress. In fiscal 1969, 2,722 began on-the-job training, working for 73 different firms, and as of January 1, 1970, nearly 6,000 Indians were participating.

As noted earlier, employers receiving subsidies provide only nominal training in some cases, though in others it is extensive. Although the average cost per individual served in fiscal 1970 was $745, most contracts specified a training period longer than one year. Hence, the average cost per placement is about $1,000. Whatever the manpower services provided, those enrolled benefit from jobs which might not otherwise be available, and almost all of which are close to or on the reservations. Given the Indians' demonstrated preference for such locations, OJT subsidies should be increased, which will in turn require that they be larger on a per enrollee basis. Few firms can be expected to locate near reservations to receive a $1,000 BIA subsidy when they can receive more than $3,000 per enrollee to locate near a ghetto and hire a usually better educated and trained group.

Components of BIA's employment assistance effort, available to all served, include programs for large families and prospective homeowners. Through a Home Purchase Program begun in July 1967, 327 Indian families had been assisted in buying a home off-reservation by the end of fiscal 1970. For families whose head is permanently employed and has a good credit rating, the BIA can provide a grant of up to $2,000 or 10 percent of the purchase price, whichever is less. With the aid of $400,000 in BIA grants, these families had purchased property worth $5,300,000. Since 1965, some 91 large (seven or more members) families have been relocated at an average cost of $2,800. This Large Family Program provides temporary income supplements to families whose head cannot earn enough but who has good potential. As his income increases, the supplements are eliminated. Through the end of fiscal 1970, over 60 percent of these families were still at the original point of relocation.

Finally, there is operated at the agency level a local placement service, primarily for temporary jobs. In fiscal 1970, nearly 4,000 placements were made; many individuals were placed in more than one job during the year. Men, who received about 85 percent of the placements, averaged $3.01 in hourly starting wages; women averaged $1.80.

Recipients of employment-assistance services in fiscal 1970 were generally young and well educated; males and single individuals predominated, and families were relatively small. However, nearly nine of every ten were unemployed when they applied for services (Table 32). And the few who were employed held low paying jobs.

Table 32. Selected Characteristics of Individuals Receiving BIA Employment Assistance Services, Fiscal 1970

	ADULT VOCATIONAL TRAINING	DIRECT EMPLOYMENT
Male	60%	76%
Female	40%	24%
Single	76%	62%
Family	24%	38%
Average number in families	3.4	4.1
Average age	23	27
Average grade level of educational achievement	11	11
On welfare at time of application	10%	14%
Unemployed at time of application	87%	89%

The record of job placements in fiscal 1970 and average starting wages indicates considerable improvement (Table 33). Although women are a minority of those served, the difference in earnings between men and women is so significant that it raises the question of whether scarce funds for manpower programs might be spent more effectively if even less were expended for women. The case for conscious discrimination by sex is buttressed by the virtual certainty that a woman's labor-force attachment will be substantially interrupted by childbearing and other family responsibilities.

An evaluation of BIA institutional and on-the-job training

Table 33. Number of Job Placements by BIA and Average
Starting Hourly Wage by Sex, Fiscal 1970*

	MEN		WOMEN	
	NUMBER	WAGE	NUMBER	WAGE
Total	3,559	$2.86	1,432	$1.99
Direct Employment				
Permanent	2,319	2.80	730	2.04
Temporary	390	3.19	64	1.72
Institutional trainees				
Permanent	790	2.92	563	1.97
Temporary	60	2.31	75	1.96

* Some individuals may have been placed more than once.
Source: Bureau of Indian Affairs.

programs in Oklahoma by Loren C. Scott and Paul R. Blume concluded that both programs resulted in significant increases in participants' annual earnings. Institutional trainees increased their pretraining earnings by slightly more than did on-the-job trainees; however, the significantly higher costs of institutional training suggest that on-the-job training may be a more effective method to upgrade the skills of American Indians.[10]

LABOR DEPARTMENT EFFORTS

Public concern about this country's disadvantaged grew during the 1960s and was enunciated in a growing series of antipoverty programs, most notably the Manpower Development and Training Act and the Economic Opportunity Act. Given the concentration of need on reservations, Indians were quite deserving of assistance from remedial education, training, and work programs.

There are a number of regular manpower programs operating on or near reservations, providing services to reservation Indians as well as those who have moved to urban areas. Nearly 24,000 Indians participated in some way, in fiscal 1970, though 13,000 were students receiving supplementary income with only nominal work and training under the Neighborhood Youth Corps (NYC) (Table 34). Available data do not distinguish Indians on reservations from those in urban areas. However, the nature of each program indicates the probable extent to which reservation Indians are involved.

Expenditures for Indians cannot be distinguished from totals. However, extrapolations based on the percentage of Indians in the various Labor Department programs suggest that about $30 million is spent for Indians; of this, probably about two-thirds—or $20 million—is spent for reservation Indians. In addition, state employment security agencies placed a number of Indians in jobs.

The most important manpower program in terms of en-

Table 34. *Indian Enrollment in Labor Department Training and Work Programs, Fiscal 1970*

PROGRAM	ESTIMATED NUMBER OF INDIANS	INDIANS AS A PERCENT OF TOTAL ENROLLMENT
Total	23,573	2.2
Manpower Development and Training		
Institutional	2,340	1.8
On-the-job	2,366	2.6
Neighborhood Youth Corps		
In school	1,786	2.4
Out-of-school	1,432	3.1
Summer	10,122	2.8
Job Opportunities in the Business Sector	694	0.8
Concentrated Employment Program	2,202	2.0
Work Incentive Program	1,205	1.3
Operation Mainstream	1,150	9.2
New Careers	76	2.1
Job Corps	200	0.5

Source: Department of Labor, Manpower Administration.

rollments is the Neighborhood Youth Corps. In-school and summer projects sponsored by the Indian Tribal Councils are designed to provide students with some work experience and training but mainly with a source of income during their school years. And the summer employment program provided employment for 10,000 students. These NYC programs have enjoyed widespread support among Indians. The income which is provided, usually at the minimum wage, is large relative to the low average family income, and the NYC tasks are not demanding. The problems are those which apply as well to the program nationally. Counseling and supervision are inadequate, and the jobs are often "make-work." The programs offer little preparation for later employment, and in fact often perpetuate reclusiveness among youth. But few doubt its value on the whole.

Out-of-school NYC employs a much smaller number of Indian youth on a year-round basis, only 630 in fiscal 1969. This program would have to be expanded drastically to serve the critical needs of young Indians who have dropped out of school, since jobs for them are almost nonexistent. But this segment of NYC is not popular among the tribes. For one thing, the minimum wage paid under the program often exceeds what is available elsewhere, and older tribal members resent the fact that dropouts can earn more than they; the high wage could conceivably encourage dropouts. The out-of-school program has also been plagued by alcoholism, absenteeism, and high drop-out rates. Despite these shortcomings, some assistance is needed for Indians who have dropped out of school, for they constitute perhaps the most serious problem group on the reservations.

Operation Mainstream is a highly popular program where it has been implemented, but through fiscal 1968, only 14 projects had been started because too little effort had been exerted by Labor Department field personnel. Mainstream is ideally suited to the needs of the reservations. It employs

mostly older Indians, whose capabilities and prospects elsewhere are meager. They are put to work in road maintenance, planting, beautification, and conservation jobs, which
require little training and in which the older Indians usually
have some experience. Little emphasis is placed on education
and training, so the program has a low cost and a high payoff
in terms of useful work which is done. Mainstream has had
problems with alcoholism among its older enrollees, and high
drop-out rates among females who leave for family reasons.
A major difficulty has been transporting participants from
their homes to work sites, and this usually has to be worked
out before a project can get underway. Despite these problems, there is little doubt that Mainstream is worthwhile,
and that it should be organized more actively on other reservations.

The other major manpower program operated on or near
reservations includes projects initiated under the Manpower
Development and Training Act (MDTA). Though MDTA has
substantial enrollments, most tribes prefer to work with
similar programs of the BIA, since they are more familiar
with the BIA's activities. Though MDTA funds for reservations are not in short supply, activity has been limited until
recently. There were only 4 regular MDTA institutional
projects designed to serve Indians in fiscal 1969, with opportunities for 282, and a special facility in Montana, the
Northwest Indian Manpower Training Center, intended to
train some 300 Indians from an 11-state area. There were
24 OJT projects also in operation in fiscal 1969, providing
subsidies of roughly $1,000 per person to private employers
to hire and train disadvantaged workers.

Participants in OJT have jobs upon completion, but there
is a serious question about the jobs for which institutional
trainees should be prepared. Under MDTA, skill shortages
must be demonstrated before training can be offered, but
there are chronic job deficiencies for the most part in or

around reservations. If MDTA is to be coordinated with economic development efforts, its policies must be made more flexible. The alternative of providing MDTA courses for job shortages in other areas is a debatable strategy. Where MDTA courses have been offered off reservations, participants have had serious financial and social problems leading to high drop-out rates. If those trained on reservations are relocated to cities, these problems are likely to occur again. The Labor Department takes the stand that there is no purpose in training for relocation on a large scale and that this will lead to more problems than it solves.

The Employment Service is playing an increasing role on the reservations, but much more needs to be done. Presently, local public employment offices employ 200 persons, 119 of whom are Indians, to work directly with the tribes. In some states these personnel have played an active role; for instance, more than 14,000 Indians were placed in non-temporary jobs during fiscal 1969 in Arizona, New Mexico, and Wyoming alone. In most states, however, the employment services have continued to ignore the needs of Indians, because they are not sure what they are supposed to be doing where job opportunities and training slots are few. Their active efforts are required as manpower programs for Indians grow, and as economic development proceeds.

Increasing attention has been given to Indians under the manpower programs administered by the Department of Labor, and based on the relative size of their population, Indians receive a disproportionate amount of funds. For instance, Indian enrollments in fiscal 1970 accounted for 2.0 percent of the Concentrated Employment Program total, 1.3 percent of the Work Incentive Program, 2.1 percent of MDTA, 2.8 percent of NYC, and 9.2 percent of the total for Operation Mainstream. In all cases, these are more than the proportion of Indians in the population. But, considering the concentration of need on the reservations, these shares still are inadequate and greater efforts must be directed toward making Indians employable, helping them to find work, and creating jobs.

In increasing the funds allocated for Indians, emphasis should be placed on upgrading, especially in public employment. A new Public Service Careers (PSC) program is being initiated which, among other things, will subsidize the costs of preparing employees in government agencies for better positions. Since so many Indians are employed by federal agencies, rather than in the private sector, efforts should be encouraged to raise the skills and responsibilities of these workers. This cannot be done without money, and the PSC is one vehicle for subsidizing upgrading costs. There is no reason why Indians should continue to hold the lowest positions in government agencies such as the BIA and IHS, which are intended to serve them. There is justification for moving Indians upward in these agencies even at the expense of non-Indian workers if they are prepared for better positions. The manpower programs should see to it that they are.

In its manpower efforts, the BIA has cordial relationships with state employment services and administrators of the Department of Labor's programs. There has been little conflict because of the obvious need for all services which can be provided, and because operations at the field level rarely overlap. Despite this cordiality, there has been little coordination, and the role of the various approaches should be spelled out. For instance, locational subsidies should perhaps be separated from OJT subsidies, with BIA being responsible for the first and the Labor Department for the second under its JOBS program, which offers flexible subsidies of more than $3,000 for OJT. Duplication which may exist between the placement services of the U.S. Employment Service and BIA should be eliminated, making the Direct Employment program focus more on those Indians who need special help, perhaps on referral from the local employment agency. The

MDTA program should be applied more actively, again, leaving Adult Vocational Training institutions to concentrate on more seriously disadvantaged Indians. Coordinated manpower services for Indians must become a reality if the original Americans are ever to become self-sufficient. Most of all, the manpower programs must be expanded along with economic development efforts so that Indians can become self-sufficient and still maintain the reservation life they hold so dear.

NOTES

1. Alan Sorkin, "Trends in Employment and Earnings of American Indians," *Toward Economic Development for Native American Communities,* Joint Economic Committee, 91st Cong., 1st Sess., 1969, vol. 1, pp. 107–108.

2. Benjamin J. Taylor and Dennis J. O'Connor, *Indian Manpower Resources in the Southwest,* Arizona State University, Tempe, 1969.

3. Alan Sorkin, "American Indians Industrialize to Combat Poverty," *Monthly Labor Review,* March 1969.

4. Small Business Administration, "Economic Development of Indian Communities: Role of the Small Business Administration," *Toward Economic Development for Native American Communities,* Joint Economic Committee, 91st Cong., 1st Sess., 1969, vol. 2, p. 378.

5. Economic Development Administration, "Indian Development Program," in ibid., p. 365.

6. U.S. Department of the Interior, Issue Support Paper No. 70-3, "Credit and Financing," Oct. 7, 1968.

7. Bureau of Indian Affairs, "Annual Credit and Financing Report," 1969, p. 19.

8. "Industry Invades the Reservation," *Business Week,* Apr. 4, 1970, pp. 72–73.

9. Joan Ablon, "American Indian Relocation: Problems of Dependency and Management in the City," *Phylon,* Winter 1965.

10. Loren C. Scott and Paul R. Blume, "Some Evidence on the Economic Effectiveness of Institutional Versus On-the-job Training," unpublished manuscript, 1970.

"I HAVE ADVISED MY PEOPLE THIS WAY: WHEN YOU FIND ANYTHING GOOD IN THE WHITE MAN'S ROAD, PICK IT UP. WHEN YOU FIND SOMETHING THAT IS BAD, OR TURNS BAD, DROP IT AND LEAVE IT ALONE." — SITTING BULL

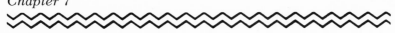

Chapter 7

Toward Indian American Communities— Without Reservations

That Indian Americans are the most deprived minority in the United States is indisputable. They are undernourished, undereducated, and underemployed; their health, housing, and community services are the worst in the country. These deplorable conditions are largely the result of mistreatment by the dominant society, and to the extent that a nation bears the guilt of its ancestors, this country has a moral obligation to help Indians solve their problems. An even more basic consideration, however, is that our society is committed to eliminating inequities by assisting those who are less fortunate. Being among the most disadvantaged of all citizens, Indians should be the target of sustained federal assistance. The isolation of Indians on reservations makes assistance feasible if effective delivery systems can be devised.

Few who are familiar with the plight of American Indians would argue against compensatory efforts to improve the conditions under which they live. Despite the rhetoric condemning the white man's neglect, the federal government has recognized its responsibility and made significant strides

Top: *Salt River Indian Agency. Mrs. Kill (Ft. McDowell Mohave-Apache) casts her ballot in the 1964 Primary Election.* Bottom: *Fancy dancers of the Plains perform their fastest and most intricate steps during the 1965 American Indian Festival, Department of the Interior, Washington, D.C.*

in recent years toward rectifying past wrongdoings. The public is becoming better informed and increasingly in agreement that something more must be done. The issue is no longer *whether* the government should increase its efforts to solve Indian problems, but *how* it should design and administer its growing assistance. And the essential question is no longer whether Custer and his modern counterparts had it coming, but whether existing government programs for Indian Americans are effectively achieving their objectives.

In education, for instance, the number of Indian students completing high school studies, matriculating in colleges and universities, and graduating from all levels of educational institutions has been increasing, however slightly. More reservation parents realize the importance of educational attainment and support various local school efforts. A few demonstration schools controlled by local communities have been established, and the number of Indian school boards helping to make the policy decisions affecting reservation schools is on the increase.

Gains in the health status of reservation Indians have been marked. Among the more significant improvements are the closing gaps between Indian and United States average life expectancies, infant and maternal mortality, and incidence of tuberculosis. Advisory boards on federal and local levels include Indian representatives, and Indian Health Service training programs are helping Indians bear increasing responsibility for the health of their own people.

Indian community action agencies funded by the Office of Economic Opportunity have demonstrated the ability of Indians to organize their own communities to work toward objectives of their own choice in a wide variety of activities. And the Bureau of Indian Affairs has supported promising experiments in community development on a few reservations. If present plans materialize, Indians on these and other reservations will administer their own communities while the federal government continues to supply the necessary resources and technical assistance.

Despite claims that many Indian natural resources are not intensely managed, government assistance has helped several reservations make constructive use of their forests. The BIA has made some successful attempts at curtailing the exploitation of Indian resources and has developed an efficient, orderly leasing procedure. Financial and data collection systems so necessary to the effective use of resources are kept in accurate detail by Bureau offices.

Through the funding of tourism, social overhead capital, and industry, several reservations have attained the economic infrastructure essential to the control of their own communities. Both the BIA and the Economic Development Administration have developed relatively viable economic areas on the Gila River reservation through the creation of industrial parks, the Warm Springs reservation through the expansion of the tourist industry, and the northeastern Navajo reservation through the establishment of a major semiconductor plant in Shiprock, New Mexico.

The Bureau of Indian Affairs has overhauled its manpower programs in recent years by forsaking the ineffective policy of stimulating migration from reservations to urban areas. The Bureau has introduced innovative family training centers to address the unique needs of helping Indians adjust to labor force requirements.

Careful analysis of the federal government's programs and policies suggests additional areas where improvements are possible and other directions in which progress is likely. Based on the lessons that have been learned, existing resources can be more effectively allocated and expanding funds can be directed toward more productive uses. But such improvements only touch the surface. The large-scale changes which must be made depend on more basic issues, ones which are highly normative and impossible to resolve in any specific manner. Social programs are ultimately based on beliefs and values that cannot be carefully tested and which must be accepted to a large extent on faith and consensus. These fundamental concepts vitally affect the design, implementation, and administration of programs; to the degree that they are ill-conceived or misdirected, the efforts themselves will suffer. In the case of Indian programs, many inadequacies are due to just such misconceptions and misdirections.

THE CONTROLLING PRINCIPLES

Five principles have been implicitly applied in the preceding analysis, and their proper implementation is vital for the success of Indian programs. First, Indians should be given the maximum feasible control over their own programs. Second, the cultural differences among Indians should be recognized and protected from erosion. Third, the living conditions on reservations—health, housing, diet, and family income—should be improved as quickly as possible. Fourth, reservation economies must be developed to support their growing populations and make them economically more self-sufficient. And fifth, the Indians must be given the option of maintaining their separateness, geographically and legally, rather than being forcibly integrated into the dominant society.

No principles such as these are without limitation or above question, and certainly their implications must be carefully considered before they serve any useful purpose. In particular, the discrepancies between these principles and past principles must be analyzed in order to determine the necessary directions of change.

1. SELF-DETERMINATION ON THE RESERVATIONS

That Indians should be given more control over their programs follows from the evidence that, in many cases, federally designed and administered efforts have failed for their lack of adaptation to Indian needs and conditions. Self-determination for its own sake is also an increasingly important goal for both social policy and those it seeks to serve. Maintaining bureaucratic obstacles to the establishment of democratic institutions is untenable since militancy has reached the reservation, and many Indians are claiming the fundamental right of self-government.

The BIA and other agencies have exercised trusteeship over Indians under the spurious belief that, without such control, Indians would make decisions inimical to their own welfare. For instance, the jurisdiction over property use was instituted and has been exercised to prevent the exploitation and expropriation of Indian lands by white men. While some tribes and individuals are able to fend for themselves, the low level of educational attainment, impoverishment, and the lack of experience with management of their resources suggest that Indians still need some federal guidance for their own protection.

Indians occupy a special position in that the federal government has legal responsibilities and powers as a result of the traditional assistance it provides to reservations. Altogether, the federal government annually spends more than half a billion dollars on Indian programs, or some $5,500 per Indian reservation family. This amount is much greater than the federal government spends per family for the rest of the population, even if all defense expenditures are included. The federal funds are allocated to programs with specific objectives, and the latitude with which they can be applied is slight, leaving no power to Indians to reallocate funds made available by the federal government.

In contrast to the stringent allocations of funds and minute regulations of their disposition on Indian reservations, other areas participating in federal programs have the power to design and implement their own projects (subject to guidelines) and to operate largely according to their own discretion. This is not true of Indian programs. While individuals who benefit from federal assistance are always subject to eligibility criteria and application procedures, only the personal lives of American Indians are regimented as a requirement for the receipt of government funds.

The goal of self-determination, therefore, does not mean complete control over the allocation and application of federal funds. Rather, it implies the same freedoms which non-Indian communities and individuals have to operate within broadly stated federal guidelines with funds allocated for separate and general purposes.

Self-determination cannot be suddenly thrust upon the tribes or upon individual Indians. Until the institutions and capabilities for self-government and administration of governmental activities are provided, the impact of sudden freedom could be disastrous. On the other hand, there is no point in creating such institutions and capabilities if meaningful freedoms are not forthcoming. Obviously, efforts to provide more viable Indian institutions and a greater ability among Indians to exercise their independence must be combined with a gradual expansion of self-determination.

Federal policy is currently moving in these directions. The Office of Economic Opportunity has taken the lead in strengthening Indian community, government, and business institutions. And some reservations have been given greater control over federal programs. For instance, according to BIA claims, the Zuñi tribe of New Mexico took over complete operational responsibility of its reservation, with a tribal governor replacing all BIA personnel. Likewise, Indians on the Salt River reservation are handling their own police force, courts, and resource development activities.

Unfortunately, the pace of change is too slow. Not enough money or effort is being expended to improve Indian abilities to operate their own programs, and control has been too gradually devolved. The BIA in particular has played a passive role, willing to grant freedom where there is demonstrated capability but doing little to encourage or help prepare Indians for self-government. Existing arrangements should not be suddenly upset, but policy should be changed so that all agencies play an *active* role in promoting greater independence. Self-determination does not have to wait until all Indians are schooled and certified to be capable of self-government or until all institutions are viable; it can be granted piecemeal and at different rates in different situations. Neither should self-determination be delayed until there is absolute proof of capability. Part of the learning process is to make mistakes, and Indians will have to have this freedom as well.

Thus, the idea that Indians should have more control over the programs which serve them does not call for a radical reorganization of traditional arrangements. It simply means that federal efforts must be intensified to strengthen Indian institutions while giving them more responsibilities and to instill capabilities while providing freedom. The pace of change must be accelerated.

2. RETAINING INDIAN CULTURES

Indian attitudes and ways of life differ markedly from those in white society and among the various tribes. There is much to be admired and much which could be learned from Indian cultures. Elements of Indian cultures and life styles that are the products of long deprivation will be eliminated as conditions change and improvements are made. The problem for both Indians and policy makers is to distinguish between those aspects which can and should be protected and those which are either anachronistic or detrimental to economic progress.

Change is unavoidable. Social programs are being implemented to improve education, diet, housing, health, community services, and economic productivity. The goals are expressed in concrete terms—lengthened school attendance, more vitamins, fewer substandard homes, reduced mortality rates, more pills to plan family size, less crime and alcoholism, more jobs, and lower unemployment rates. Few would argue with these goals or want them to be restricted for fear of adversely affecting culture or life style. And there is no doubt that existing programs for Indians will lead to drastic improvements in their measurable standards of living.

Where possible, however, these programs must be adjusted to allow for and protect differences and to reduce the cataclysmic impact of change. This may mean sustaining institutions and beliefs that have little applicability under improved conditions. For instance, Indian medicine men can be used by the IHS in delivering some of its services, or Indian court systems can be used as the foundation on which a legal system more suited to an economically developed and highly populated area can be built. In other respects, programs should be designed to protect those aspects of Indian cultures which are basic. For example, economic development programs must take care not to break down the familial systems and living patterns of Indians. Specifically, more jobs must be created for male family heads than for women in order to maintain family stability, and transportation systems must be provided so that Indians will not have to move from sparsely populated areas in order to find jobs. The love of nature and attachment to the land which are dominant characteristics of Indian cultures demand care in the development of natural resources; since most reservations remain unpolluted, conservation measures can be applied *before* problems develop so that the reservations will not be despoiled.

There are also some aspects of Indian cultures which must be changed, since they offer little of value and are obstacles to improvement. For instance, inheritance practices are clearly out of date because a growing population has made multiple ownership highly impractical. Primogeniture or some other method of solving the heirship problem is needed so that land resources can be effectively utilized. Likewise, many economic practices must be changed. While skills and crafts should be maintained as a cultural heritage, they are rarely an economic asset. Efforts to open pottery, archery, fishhook, and moccasin factories on reservations in order to utilize "special Indian skills" are misleading, for they usually only lead to Indian mass production of articles formerly made by skilled craftsmen.

These are of necessity very general indications of the adjustments which must be made. The fact is that the differences in culture and life style among tribes are almost as great as those between Indians and white society. Some tribes have almost totally adopted the white man's culture, while others have maintained a remarkable degree of their own unique life style. No hard and fast rules can dictate the adjustments that should be made in public policy. But flexibility is clearly needed, and the best way to ensure it is to increase the degree of tribal authority over the decisions that are made. More than for any other group, the differences among Indians demand a decentralization of decision making and control.

3. IMPROVING THE STANDARDS OF INDIAN LIVING

Statistics comparing living conditions on reservations with national averages reveal the Indians to be our most deprived minority. There is no doubt that their health, housing, diet, education, and economic welfare are far below what most would consider minimal levels. There is an obvious need for immediate corrective action. However, it is important that realizable goals be set. This implies that meaningful standards of adequacy should be determined and that the rate of progress be regulated to that change will become constructive rather than destructive.

Society's commitment is to secure equal opportunities for all people and to provide minimal assistance levels to those in need so that self-improvement will be possible. In health, education, manpower, and economic development, Indians are receiving a greater per capita share of funds than the rest of the nation and probably more than the average received by all other poor people.

What makes conditions worse for Indians is that they are concentrated in particular areas with limited access to more affluent economies and public facilities. Ghetto residents suffering from the worst forms of discrimination can take advantage of economic and cultural opportunities throughout the city and can benefit from and utilize its school system and other social capital. Indians, on the other hand, are cut off by their cultural differences, their special legal status, and their geographic isolation. Thus, they lack the normal opportunities to improve their economic status. Not only are Indians destitute, but they are isolated and trapped in their poverty.

The standards of Indian life can be improved by raising federal contributions, but Indians have no more claim to scarce federal resources than other similarly disadvantaged persons. What they can rightly claim, however, are resources that will equalize their opportunities and help them improve their own conditions. Success should not be measured in terms of adequate food allowances, public housing units, federally funded health facilities and employment slots—

though all important—but rather in terms of the Indians' ability to provide for their own needs. Thus, priorities and high standards for Indians should be assigned to programs which promise to equalize opportunity and eliminate the causes of poverty. This suggests greater concentration of funds for higher education, manpower, and economic development and more modest additional outlays for health, housing, food, and welfare.

In realizing any goals, care must be taken that the resulting changes do not become too disruptive. It is, of course, difficult to determine the adaptability of a people to changes in their life style. There is no doubt that some tribes and individual Indians can successfully interact with the larger society and participate in the "economic mainstream." Others will fail or will become alienated by a forced injection. The pace of change must be carefully determined and must be set by the people who are affected. It must be recognized, however, that assistance offered will act inexorably as agents of change; by accepting aid, change is forced upon Indian society. If standards of living are raised through increased federal assistance, the willingness of tribes and individuals to go it alone is reduced. Added educational attainment may generate desire for faster change among the better-educated Indians, while those who are older or more disadvantaged will understandably resist such change. Economic development is not usually accomplished by a democratic process, but rather by the decisive leadership of the few who value its benefits more than the conventional means of making a living. In the case of Indians, the federal government and tribal councils must spearhead these activities, even if they have to take steps unpopular among those who value the old style of life. An effort must be made to publicize the benefits of development, to assure that they will not be undermined by immediate offsets to assistance, and to help those victims of change.

4. ECONOMIC DEVELOPMENT OF THE RESERVATION

The key to self-determination and a higher standard of living is economic development. Unless industrial and commercial enterprises are located on or near the reservations so that jobs and earnings are available, Indians will necessarily continue as wards of the state or will have to migrate from their homesteads.

The means to economic development are not as obvious as the needs. Reservations vary widely in their states of and potentials for development. Nevertheless, there are two general characteristics of the development process that have widespread implications. First, for reservations as well as other areas, investments in economic development can be easily dissipated with little lasting effect unless the level of investment is adequate to generate further growth and expansion to enable those helped to become self-sustaining. Second, economic development requires abstinence on the part of those living in the developing area. Savings must be increased and then invested, and investments with a longer-run return must be stressed.

The first point suggests that economic development funds must be concentrated on those reservations which are closest to reaching the takeoff point. By the same token, an equitable distribution of limited funds means that resources will be frittered away in projects with only a slight long-run impact. Equity or need alone should not be the determinants of resource allocations; rather the potential of the reservation to sustain economic growth should be the most crucial selective factor. This selective rationing is difficult to implement since all areas will press their claim for development, but it is a decision which must be made. Different criteria must apply to public assistance for which all districts have equal claim and for economic development, which should be extended only to those who can take advantage of federal help.

The second prerequisite of economic development is that

tribes must be persuaded to use more of their own resources for this purpose. Development requires that they defer the benefits of economic improvement. There is no doubt that tribal councils must play a major role in these decisions since they are likely to act as the agents for the development efforts. At the same time, the federal government can effect "forced savings" by allocating increased funds to economic development efforts in lieu of other programs to improve Indian welfare. This is also a difficult decision; but unless it is done, Indians on many reservations may never mount the scale of abstinence and investment which is required.

5. MAINTAINING THE SPECIAL STATUS OF INDIANS

There is continuing debate over the future status of Indians. At one extreme are those who claim that federal responsibilities should be terminated, the reservations divided up among their residents, and Indians assimilated into the economic and social mainstream. At the other extreme, there are those who argue that the present relationship between Indians and the federal government should not be altered, that federal assistance should expand along existing lines, and that Indian separateness should be protected at all costs.

Indian policy has wavered between these extremes. In the 1950s several reservations were "terminated" and their special status removed while BIA policy, with congressional prodding, was emphasizing the relocation of Indians to urban areas. The decided failure of both efforts led to a shift in policy in the middle 1960s. The new thrust called for the deemphasis of relocation and a refutation of any intention to seek termination.

Current policies stress the economic development of reservations with the promise of improved standards of living and self-sufficiency, while at the same time disclaiming any move toward "termination." In a sense, this presents the tenuous notion that present relationships will continue after economic improvement and increased freedom.

Despite the complicated legal foundations of the Indians' status, their position is essentially determined by the facts that they are subject to government controls and are the beneficiaries of special efforts. Federal assistance will no doubt be reduced as Indians utilize self-determination and their overall conditions improve. When tribes develop to the point where they can make it on their own, they can choose between continued trusteeship or self-determination; under such conditions special status will no longer be a problem.

However, problems will arise in the development process before self-determination and self-sufficiency become a reality. Some Indians will favor complete freedom, while others will want to retain government supervision during this process. The exercise of choice is not as simple as it may seem. For instance, individual Indians are now being granted control over their property as they are adjudged to be "competent." They can develop or sell their holdings as they see fit, though their action may undermine the use of reservation land remaining in trust status. Another difficulty is the problem of those who have left the reservation. Many living elsewhere are still tribal members with full rights, but their needs and preferences may be entirely different from those who are living on the reservation. Residents may favor the use of tribal income for economic development while those living elsewhere might prefer its direct distribution.

Such difficulties are not easily overcome. But the decision whether or not to remain under BIA jurisdiction should clearly be made by those who are living on the reservation. For those who leave, some other settlement might be arranged. Self-determination must prevail, but care must be taken to structure the choice so that real freedom is exercised.

IMPROVING INDIAN PROGRAMS

The federal government performs the same functions and provides similar programs and services for the entire United States population as it does for reservation Indians. While the particular form of the Indian programs is unique and the assistance more extensive, the provisions of education, manpower, health care, resource development, social welfare, community organization, and economic development are included in the government's responsibility for all American citizens. And just as decisions must be made regarding the content of these programs for the benefit of the entire country, so must they be made for Indian programs. No exact prescriptions flow from the general controlling principles, but combined with the lessons of success and failure under the Indian programs and with some understanding of the Indian problems, they can serve as a basis for considering improvements in all areas of federal activity. These suggestions indicate some ways in which federal funds could be spent for a more potent impact.

1. EDUCATION

In order to achieve the ultimate goal of providing Indian children equal educational opportunities, public education and "Indian" education must become real and viable alternatives. School facilities available to reservation residents, whether they be located in nearby towns and cities or directly on the reservation, need to provide adequate educational backgrounds suited to the particular needs of Indian students, enabling them to function productively in American society.

Equality of educational opportunities means that public schools should be available to reservation children whenever possible. To help encourage Indian enrollment, public schools might provide the meals and health care currently available in the boarding schools. Federal funds should be made available to local school districts near reservations for the improvement of their offerings to Indian pupils and to compensate for the extra costs entailed in educating these children. Curricula, texts, and other instructional materials must be revised to meet the needs and backgrounds of Indian children, and local Indians could be used as teacher aides, storytellers, and arts and crafts instructors.

A primary prerequiste for the attainment of an equal and integrated school system is a deemphasis on boarding school education. Boarding schools are expensive, with relatively few demonstrated benefits, and should be restricted to only severely isolated or homeless children.

Indian communities should be encouraged to assume control over their schools and to utilize the talents of local personnel to plan and administer community schools based on the values, needs, and norms of both traditional culture and that of the dominant society. In place of the highly centralized BIA educational system, locally controlled school systems are likely to be responsive to the uniqueness and needs of each reservation community.

2. HEALTH CARE

All available health indices indicate that reservation populations are far behind the rest of the nation, although the medical services offered by the Indian Health Service are better than those available to most rural populations. Many of the causes lie outside the realm of better medicine. But health can be improved through increased stress on the prevention of disease and disability through education.

In health, as in education, Indians should have an increased voice in the determination and implementation of policies. In order for traditional professional attitudes and medical procedures to become more adapted to and accepted by the Indian community, Indians must become involved in all aspects of health care. Training should be expanded and Indian personnel employed on all levels of delivery—from federal health boards to nurses' aides and laboratory technicians. Health service personnel can benefit from the counsel of tribal leaders, medicine men, and local health boards.

3. WELFARE

Considering the low average family income of Indians, any increase in welfare payments could have a massive effect. The Family Assistance Plan (FAP) and other proposals for a guaranteed income could therefore substantially improve conditions on the reservation. For instance, the average Indian family, which had four members in 1968, had earnings of roughly $2,200 from wages and salaries. Under FAP, a family of four would be eligible for a $1,600 basic payment; each dollar of earnings over $60 per month would be "taxed" at a rate of 50 percent. Thus, an Indian family of four would receive a payment of $740 while keeping its $2,200 earnings. Food stamps would further raise the real income of the family.

Care must be exercised, however, that increased welfare payments do not permanently damage work incentives. The idea behind FAP is that even when a family is being subsidized, it will have good reason to work. But Indians have less work experience, less opportunity to work, and probably less incentive, so their already low labor-force participation rates might decline when an income is guaranteed that would almost support their current life styles without work. If FAP is enacted, the impact of the guaranteed income on Indian work incentive should be closely scrutinized.

4. NATURAL RESOURCE DEVELOPMENT

Several changes are needed if Indians are to realize the full benefits of their resource endowments. Most fundamentally, more extensive and more detailed surveys must be made of the reservation resources which obviously cannot be developed until they are discovered. The BIA, the Geodetic Survey, and the tribes should all increase their efforts in these directions.

The BIA must also play a more active role in promoting Indian interests. On farm and ranch lands in particular, Indians are realizing only a small proportion of their potential income. The best lands are frequently rented at below market rates. Though the government does not and should not dictate how Indians use their lands, BIA officials can intensify appraisal services and expand technical assistance to induce more efficient operations of Indian resources.

One area needs special emphasis. Indian water rights have gradually been eroded or their potential left undeveloped. This has been due to the BIA's failure to stand up for Indians, and outright aggrandizement by other agencies. The expropriation of Indian water rights is a manifestation of continuing mistreatment by the white man.

5. DEVELOPING HUMAN AND ECONOMIC RESOURCES

In the area of manpower, intensive remedial services for Indian youth should be expanded, with special emphasis placed upon institutional training programs. Public employment of the elderly should be expanded and directed toward much-needed labor-intensive projects, such as the construction and maintenance of roads, sewage systems, and parks. Most importantly, the manpower programs of the BIA must be coordinated with those of the Department of Labor to minister to the unique needs of the Indian population.

Economic development funds and programs should be

concentrated on those reservations with the most potential for self-support in terms of trained and available manpower, the existence of natural resources, and developed social and political institutions. Additional funds are sorely needed for the establishment of commercial enterprises in reservation areas, and Indians should be encouraged to develop tribally owned enterprises. But before progress can be made on most reservations, their infrastructures must be improved to support increased industrialization; reservation transportation systems in particular need drastic improvement. Locational subsidies to attract private firms to developing reservations should also be increased and coordinated with manpower training subsidies.

TREATING CAUSES RATHER THAN SYMPTOMS

To meet all the needs of reservation Indians, resources would have to be substantially increased. Some improvements can be accomplished through reallocations of resources, but reallocations are difficult to engineer unless funds are increasing. The key, as in the solution of most social problems, is more money and the more intelligent use of existing money.

It is likely that the resources committed to solving Indian problems will increase as the public becomes more aware of their plight. But it is improbable that the forthcoming funds will be adequate to meet all demands. It will be necessary to make difficult choices between competing claimants and to determine priorities on the basis of rational analysis.

Though all eggs should never be put in one basket, one area of activity should clearly be given highest priority. The primary goal of Indian programs is to increase Indian control over their own destinies and to improve their standard of living. The *sine qua non* to achieve both of these goals is the development of reservation economies.

The potential benefits of economic development are pervasive. For one thing, self-determination can be achieved only when a population rises out of economic dependency. Regardless of the form in which federal funds are given to the reservation—whether through BIA allocations or block grants—they are still controlled by the United States government and its agencies. Indians need to eliminate special federal assistance to be able to exercise maximum control over their own affairs. Once they can produce their own sources of funding, they can be free of unsolicited advice, guidelines, restrictions, and stipulations imposed by Washington agencies.

Multiple benefits are likely to flow from economic development. The close correlation between income and education, for instance, is well documented. The scholastic performance of children living on meager welfare is bound to suffer. A community's command of adequate resources allows its members to decide the form and content of education that is best suited to their own children's needs and to be able to implement their decisions. To the degree that economic development stimulates added income and self-sufficiency, it will also improve educational attainment.

A significant proportion of disease and premature death among Indians is a direct result of poverty, dilapidated housing, unsanitary water, and inadequate diets. A sound economy would mean that the necessary resources would be available to both the tribal community and individual families to build adequate housing, purchase nutritional foods, and construct sanitation facilities. Schools and communities could offer health education programs, and individuals would have the financial ability to follow their recommendations for better health care.

With economic development, the number of Indians dependent upon welfare would also decrease. For those not benefiting from increased economic opportunities, more intensive services and substantial assistance could be provided. Another potential benefit is that as Indians take on more responsibilities and are trained for meaningful jobs, they will become increasingly qualified for technical, managerial, and supervisory positions.

Despite the advantages of economic development, it is unrealistic to suppose that all reservation communities can benefit. Some reservations have limited potential, and a concentration of funds is required for these to have much effect. To distribute funds equally among all tribes would be to dissipate them on minor projects with limited impact. While allowing only a few reservations the resources to develop their economies seems inequitable, those who cannot be immediately helped will be no worse off than they are presently, and eventually resources will be available in increased quantity for their needs.

The best choice of reservations would be those most likely to meet with successful development. These would be communities with available natural and manpower resources, strong internal organizations, and functioning self-governments. Since one of the major problems in developing the economy of any community is the coordination of all its institutions, it might be helpful to choose reservations that already exercise some control over education, health, community organization, welfare, and other features of local life. The presence of this partial self-determination would increase the likelihood that local control over the use of funds could be effected early in the program. A nearby town or city with knowledgeable and willing expertise in industry, business, and factory skills would also enhance the chances of success and might open important areas of interdependency between the reservation and the white community. At the outset, the probability of success may be more important than the existence of need, for the political support so essential for the funding of any government program is more likely to come with success than with sincere attempts.

Past experience has indicated that a growing and productive economy is the single most important factor in the better-
ment of a population's social institutions. While this is not the
only approach that can be taken to improve the conditions
on Indian reservations, it does seem to be the most promising.
And the right combination of Indian participation with federal assistance can provide the economic independence so
necessary to provide Indians control over their own destinies.
Viable economies make viable communities, and self-determination requires self-sufficiency.

ADMINISTRATION OF PROGRAMS

While the ultimate goal for Indian communities is self-determination through self-sufficiency, the present issue is where
the responsibility for decisions regarding reservation programs and the control of federal funds for these programs
should lie. A common denominator of most programs discussed thus far is that they were planned and conceived in
Washington. As the programs are all administered by the
BIA or other federal agencies, the Indians have been the
passive recipients of the federal aid and have had little to
do with determining the scope or direction of the programs.
Except for an occasional official who made it to the higher
rungs of the bureaucracy, few reservation Indians have
participated in planning Indian programs. By the time any
funds arrive at the reservation, they are carefully earmarked
and their disposition predetermined. The recipients of the
program lack authority to reallocate funds or are denied
discretion in expending the allocated resources. Washington
determines what is good for the Indians, and the Indians
can take it or leave it. BIA's officialdom in the field has
shared the same frustrations with their Indian clients. A
school principal with a million-dollar budget, for instance,
lacks discretionary authority and must wallow in layers of

red tape before he can buy another piece of chalk or order a textbook if it has not been allotted in the budget.

Any government agency that has been in business for more than seven score years is bound to suffer from the hardening of its bureaucratic arteries. And even the BIA's best friends wouldn't argue that it is an exception. While blaming the BIA or other federal bureaucracies for the problems of the Indians is a popular sport, it is of little help to the Indians. Suggestions to abolish the BIA and to distribute its functions among various federal agencies are likely to bring more fragmentation of the limited help offered to Indians and to result in greater waste rather than improved services. Some have proposed that the activities of the BIA be distributed on a functional basis. This approach would give the Office of Education responsibility for schooling the nation's Indian children, the Labor Department the task of training the Indian work force, the Department of Housing and Urban Development the job of providing adequate housing, and so on. Such a dispersion of activity and assistance would make it even more difficult for Indians to determine program priorities, even if the federal agencies would decide to relinquish authority to tribal councils.

Indian reservations should have maximum latitude in determining the allocation of federal resources within broad federal guidelines. Similarly, these guidelines should be prepared by the agencies responsible for the programs with the continuing cooperation of representatives from Indian reservations. Federal officials would then concentrate on monitoring projects to ascertain whether federal objectives are being followed and on offering technical expertise in effectively administering projects funded by the federal government. This is in line with both the "creative federalism" favored by the Great Society and the "new federalism" urged by the Nixon administration.

One of the most significant accomplishments of "creative

federalism" was the passage of the Economic Opportunity Act of 1964 which attempted to encourage local initiative through direct grants to Indian groups and permitted them to initiate programs and organize their operational structure. Tribal councils were encouraged to run their own affairs rather than turn for "guidance" to federal officials. For the first time in the long history of the federal government playing Big Brother to the Indians did the federal agency defer to the Indians to let them develop their own community programs. Without passing judgment upon the wisdom of individual projects sponsored with Office of Economic Opportunity funds, other federal agencies might adapt the lessons learned from OEO by allowing reservation Indians a greater say in developing their own institutions. The Indians themselves must determine whether they want to join the way of living of the majority or continue with their own traditional institutions.

The OEO experience suggests the need of offering the Indians the opportunity not only to design and administer their own programs but also to participate in the determination of priorities in allocating limited resources. Such changes in the disposition of funds can be brought about only by congressional action removing the stringent earmarking of funds appropriated for Indian programs. The reorganization of the executive agencies alone will not allow the Indians a greater degree of freedom in administering their own programs.

President Nixon strongly supported Indian self-determination as a major thrust of his "new federalism" in a message on Indian affairs delivered in July, 1970. He addressed himself to a new national policy of strengthening "the Indian's sense of autonomy without threatening his sense of community" and rejected the extreme measures of both forced termination and federal paternalism. To facilitate maximum Indian responsibility for the administration of service programs, the President announced proposed legislation to enable any tribe or Indian community to take over the control and operation of federally funded programs within the Departments of Interior and Health, Education, and Welfare. Realizing that the ability to sustain these programs ultimately depends upon the development of an Indian infrastructure, he additionally proposed an "Indian Financing Act of 1970" to extend the existing Revolving Loan Fund that lends capital for economic development projects and provides additional interest subsidies, loan insurance, and guarantees to encourage the support of conventional lenders for Indian projects. To help make Indian communities more competitive in attracting the capital for recreational, industrial, and commercial enterprises, President Nixon suggested that legislation be enacted to offer tribes long-term leases on their property. Further, it was recommended that more tribes follow the example of the Zuñi and Salt River reservations in developing comprehensive economic plans. He concluded that the most effective way in which to improve Indian programs is to intimately involve those persons most affected by the programs—the residents of the various reservations.

An important implication for federal officials connected with programs under the "new federalism" approach is the recognition that the cultural heritage of the native Americans does not easily fall into the mold of guidelines designed for a competitive society that cherishes the values of the Protestant ethic. This means that Indian programs must be in harmony with their cultural traditions, and what is good for General Motors is not necessarily good for Indians. Appropriate Indian programs must also recognize that there is great diversity among Indian tribes and that projects that are helpful on one reservation may not be appropriate for all Indian tribes.

According to this approach, a given tribe could choose among viable alternatives for the delivery of a certain service. For instance, a tribal council or other elected authority could decide to use educational funds to reimburse a neighboring public school if the Indian parents want to send their children to that school; or they could send some of the children to a BIA boarding school and organize their own community school for the others.

The goal of Indian self-determination should be the ultimate withering away of "special" federal programs. But the independence of Indian reservations will have to await the development of the needed infrastructure which would make it possible for Indian communities to be able to support their own institutions as other parts of the United States are doing. Paradoxically, if Indians living on reservations are ever to be discontinued as "wards of the state," increased federal aid would be necessary to help reservations develop their economic base and social institutions. Moreover, vested interests in tribal councils are likely to oppose any changes which would infringe upon their powers. But the increased help must be accompanied by an emphasis upon democratic control over these developing institutions, and the aid, which must be in line with diverse Indian needs and values, may not necessarily be kosher for white society.

INDEX

776 09/01   71
     18279